TRACING LETTERS

ASL Handwriting Book

www.mamaishere.com

"We must find time to stop and thank the people who make a difference in our lives."
- John F. Kennedy

So, I would like to say: THANK YOU!

Hi! I used to be a nanny when I was a teenager, then a tutor and a teacher (at the same time I got my Bachelor's Degree in Design) . Nowadays, I am a designer and a mom - or how I like to call it: mama). This is how "Mama Is Here" was born!

I hope I am making a difference in your children's lives and thank you for making one in mine!

If you love this product, please consider leaving a positive review! Feel free to check our shop for similar products (:

@mamaishere2021

follow to check daily activities you can do with your little one!

Text and illustration © Copyright 2022 Writerverse Journey
Book Design by Kelle Lima a.k.a. Mama Is Here

ISBN: 979-8-9857051-4-0

Published in 2022 by Writerverse Journey LLC, in Salt Lake City, UT, USA. All rights reserved.

Dear Teachers & Parents,

This pencil control book contains 26 letters of the alphabet (A-Z) with American Sign Language support.

The letters are not introduced in a conventional ABC order: instead they were arranged in an attempt to teach your child from simpler (easier to draw letters) to more complex hand movements.

Each letter is written by using a geometric basic shape, or by putting multiple ones together.

I hope I'm providing your kid the ability to recognize and write letters in both lowercase and uppercase as well as their respective signs (hand gestures)!

Thank you again and have fun!

Cheers,
Kelle Lima

Check out other books from "Little Fingers" series, such as:

>

TRACING NUMBERS:
ASL Handwriting Book

THIS IS THE LETTER "O": TRACE IT WITH YOUR FINGER

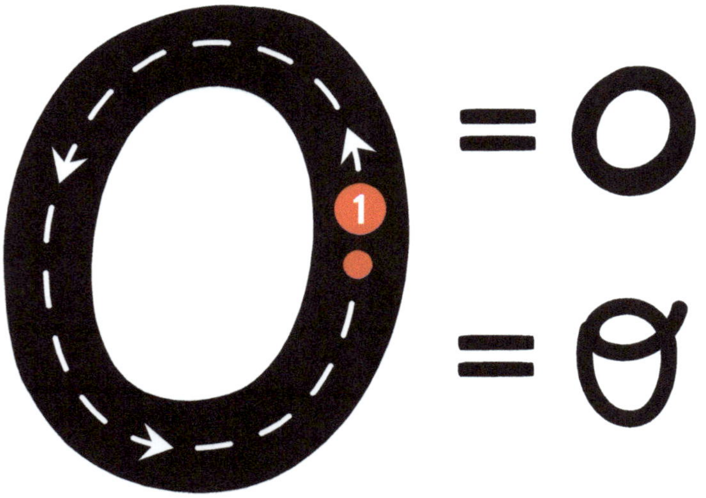

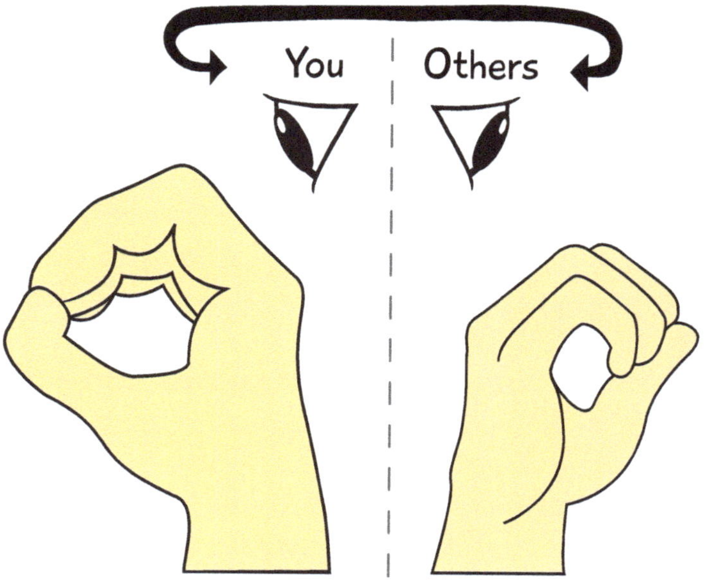

O = O

O = o

You | Others

Owl

Ocean

Orange

Onion

Oatmeal

Trace the dotted lines with a pencil or pen to finish the picture!

Let's practice the letter "O" now!

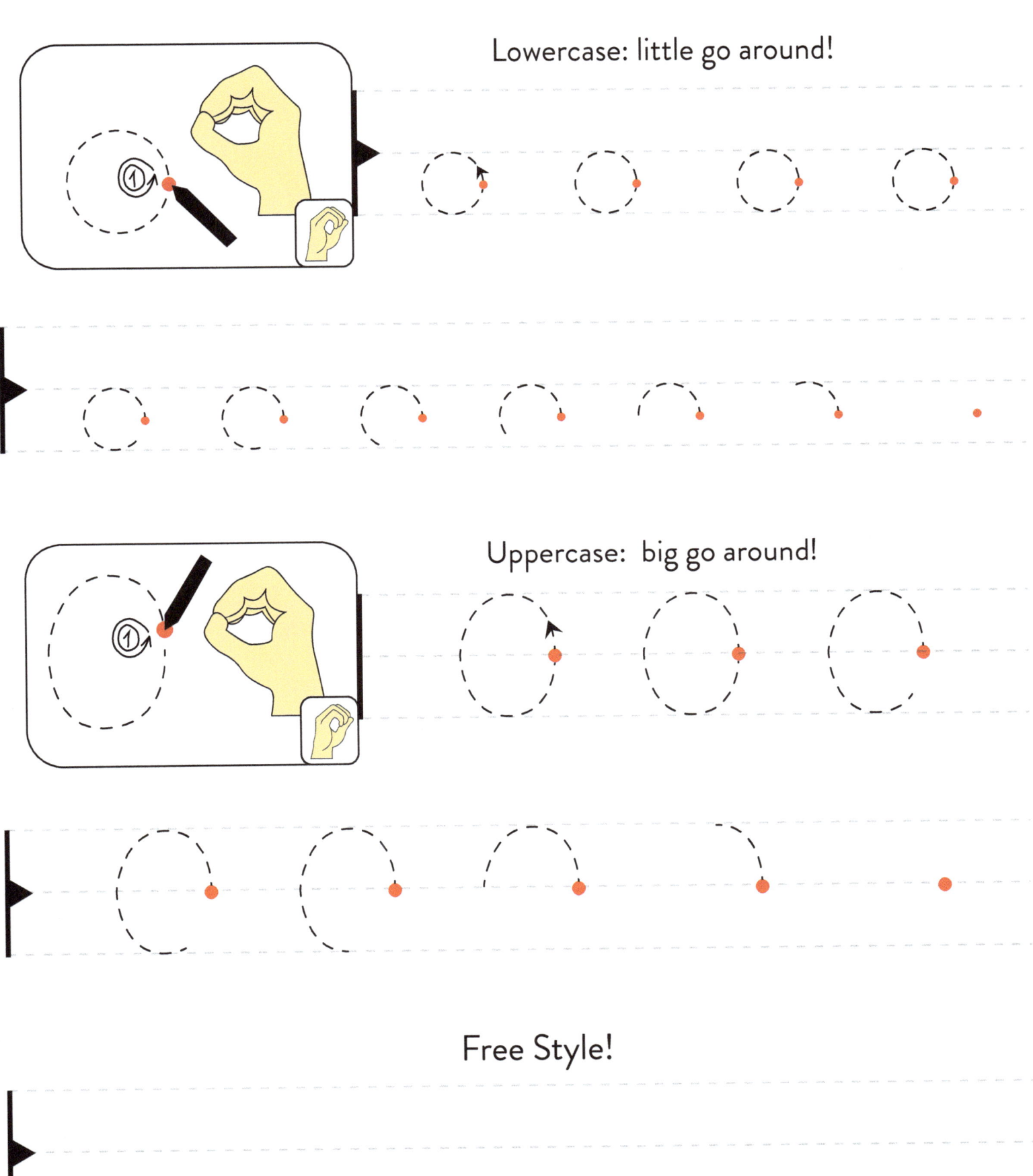

Lowercase: little go around!

Uppercase: big go around!

Free Style!

THIS IS THE LETTER "L": TRACE IT WITH YOUR FINGER

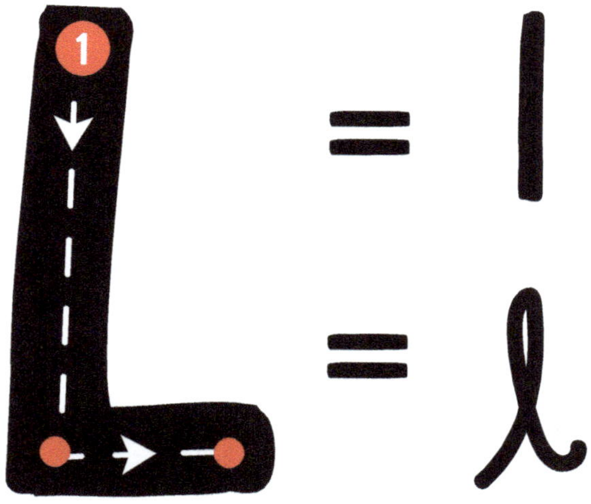

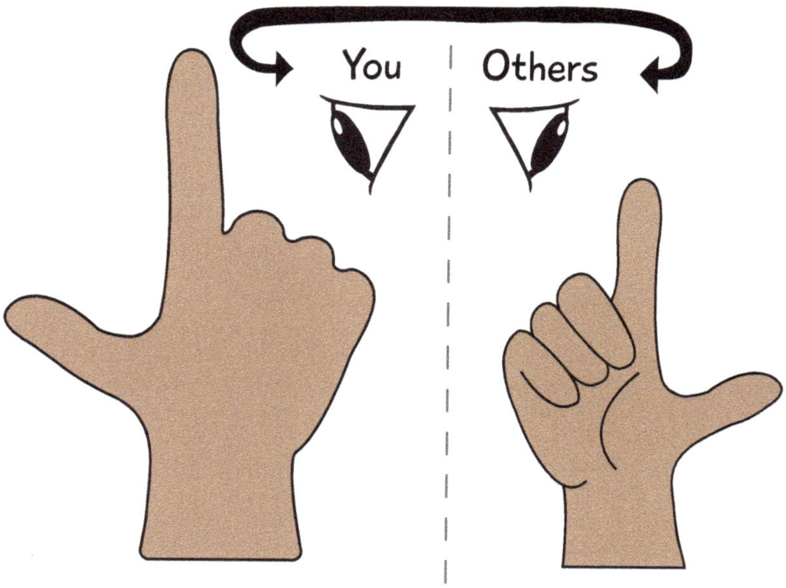

L = l
L = ℓ

You | Others

Lion   Little   Leopard

Lunch   Leaf

Trace the dotted lines with a pencil or pen to finish the picture!

Let's practice the letter "L" now!

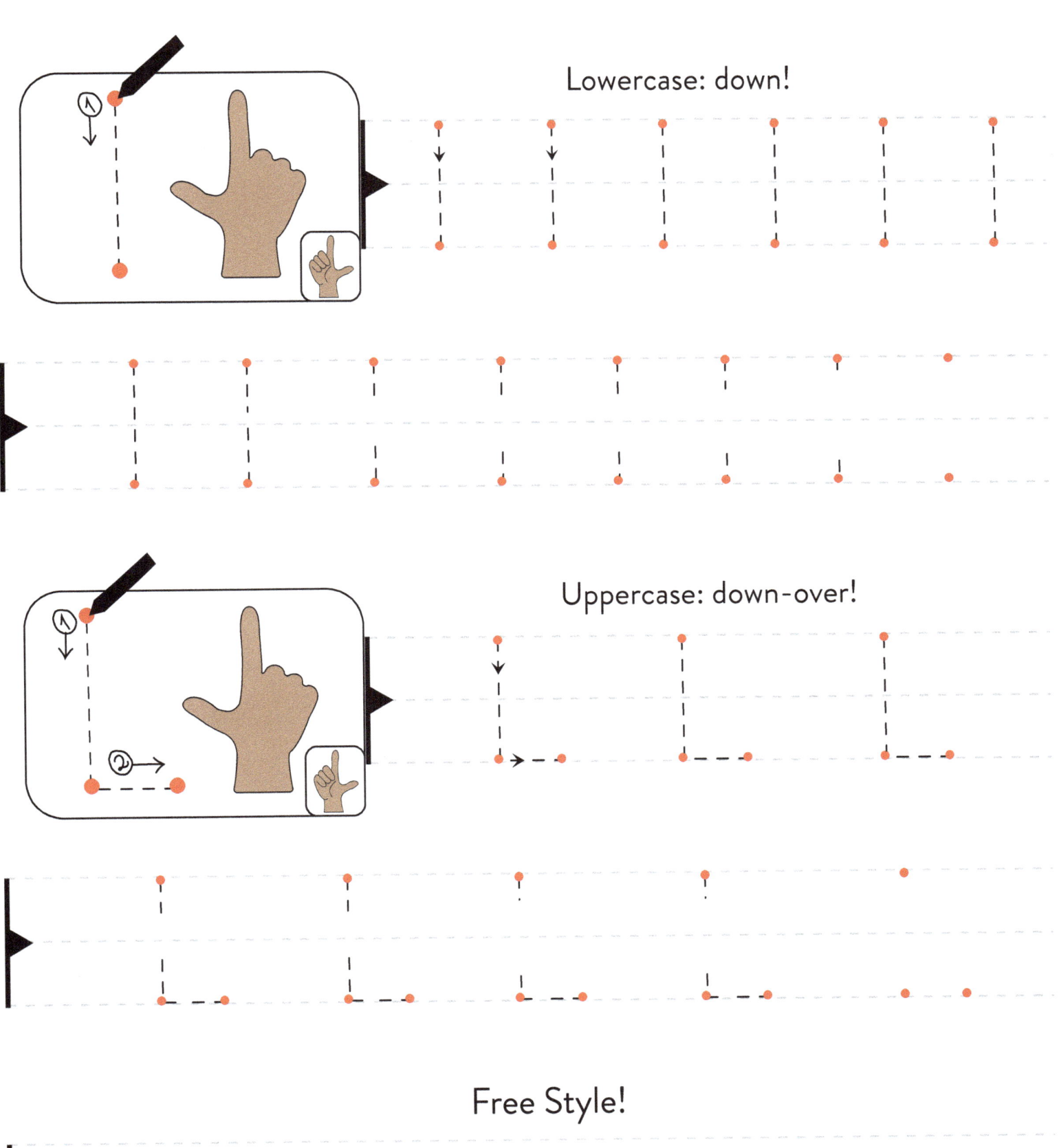

Lowercase: down!

Uppercase: down-over!

Free Style!

THIS IS THE LETTER "A": TRACE IT WITH YOUR FINGER

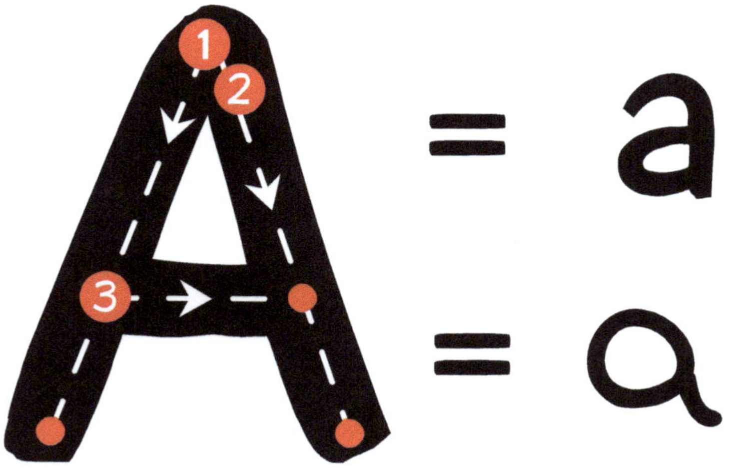

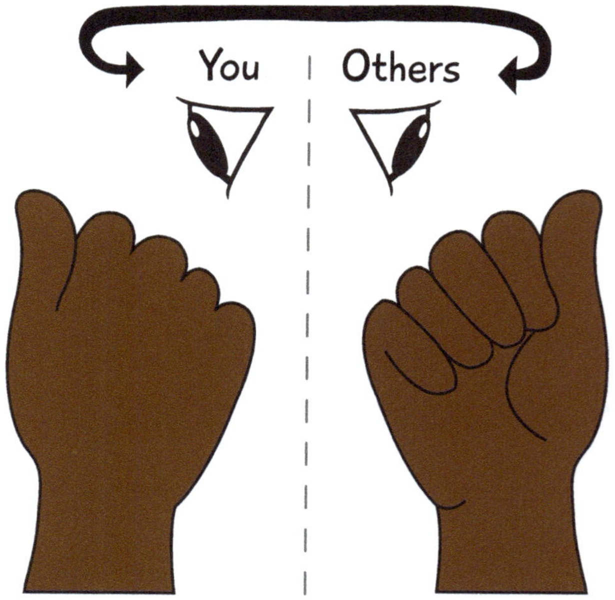

A = a

A = a

You | Others

Apple

Alligator

Amazing

Angry

Airplane

Trace the dotted lines with a pencil or pen to finish the picture!

Let's practice the letter "A" now!

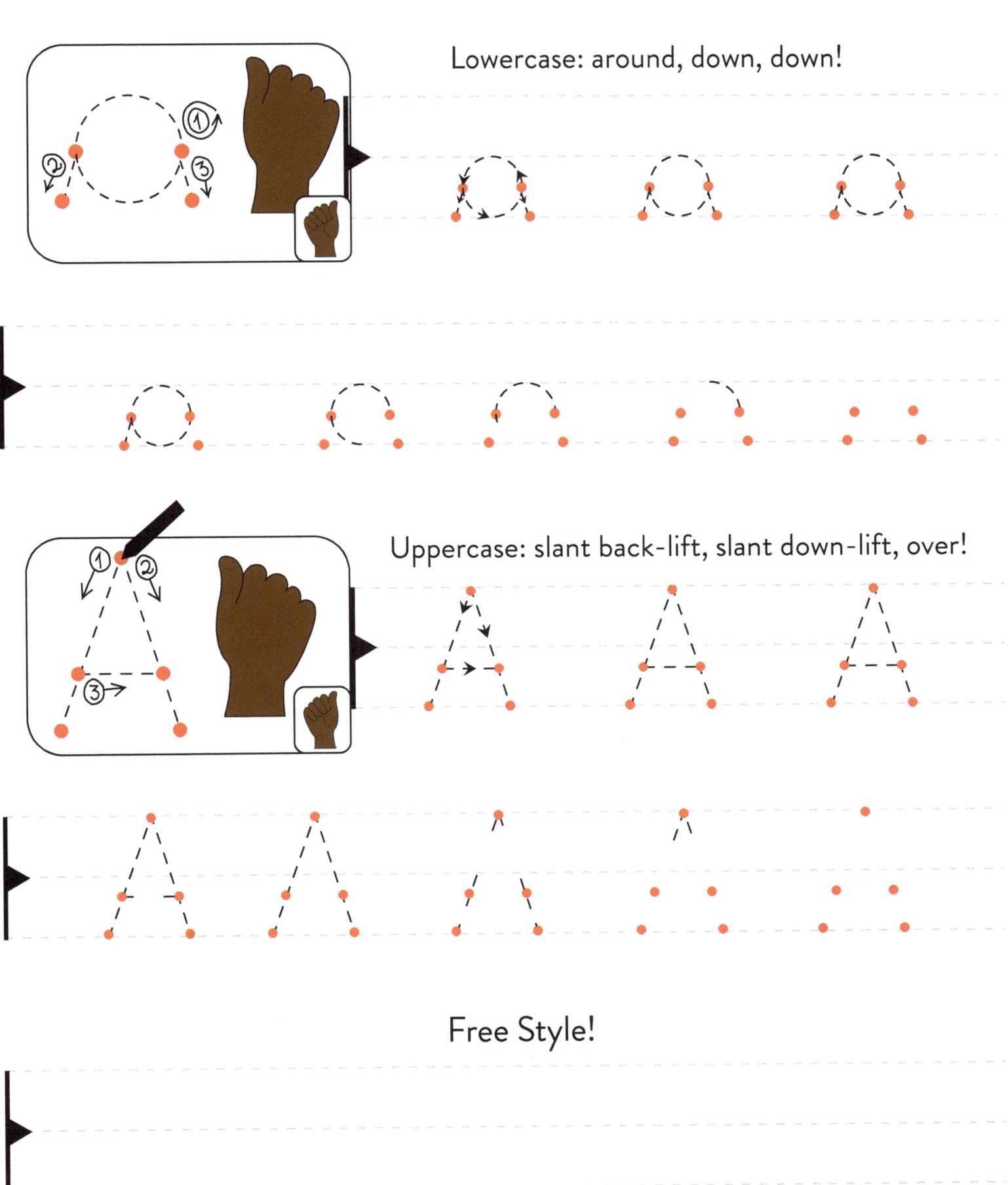

Lowercase: around, down, down!

Uppercase: slant back-lift, slant down-lift, over!

Free Style!

THIS IS THE LETTER "T": TRACE IT WITH YOUR FINGER

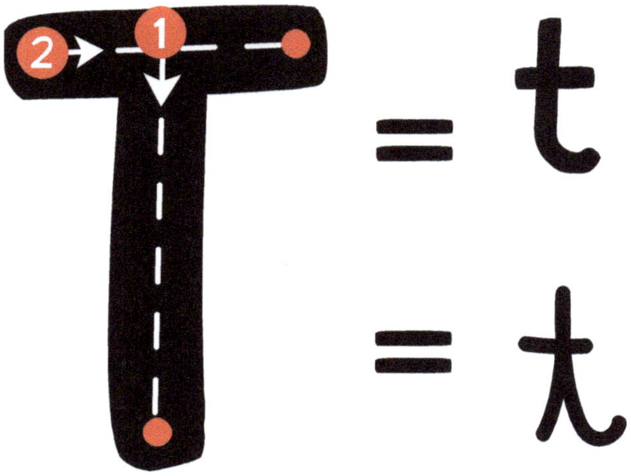

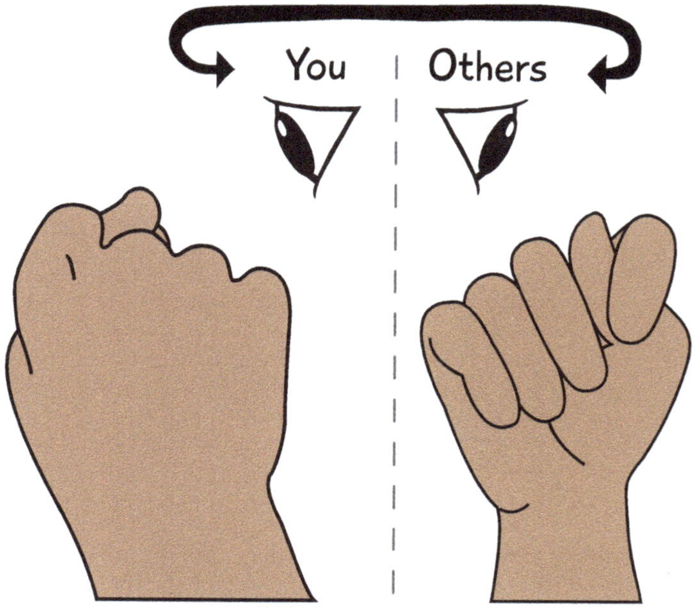

T = t

T = t

You | Others

Tree

Tiger

Tent

Two

Tomato

Trace the dotted lines with a pencil or pen to finish the picture!

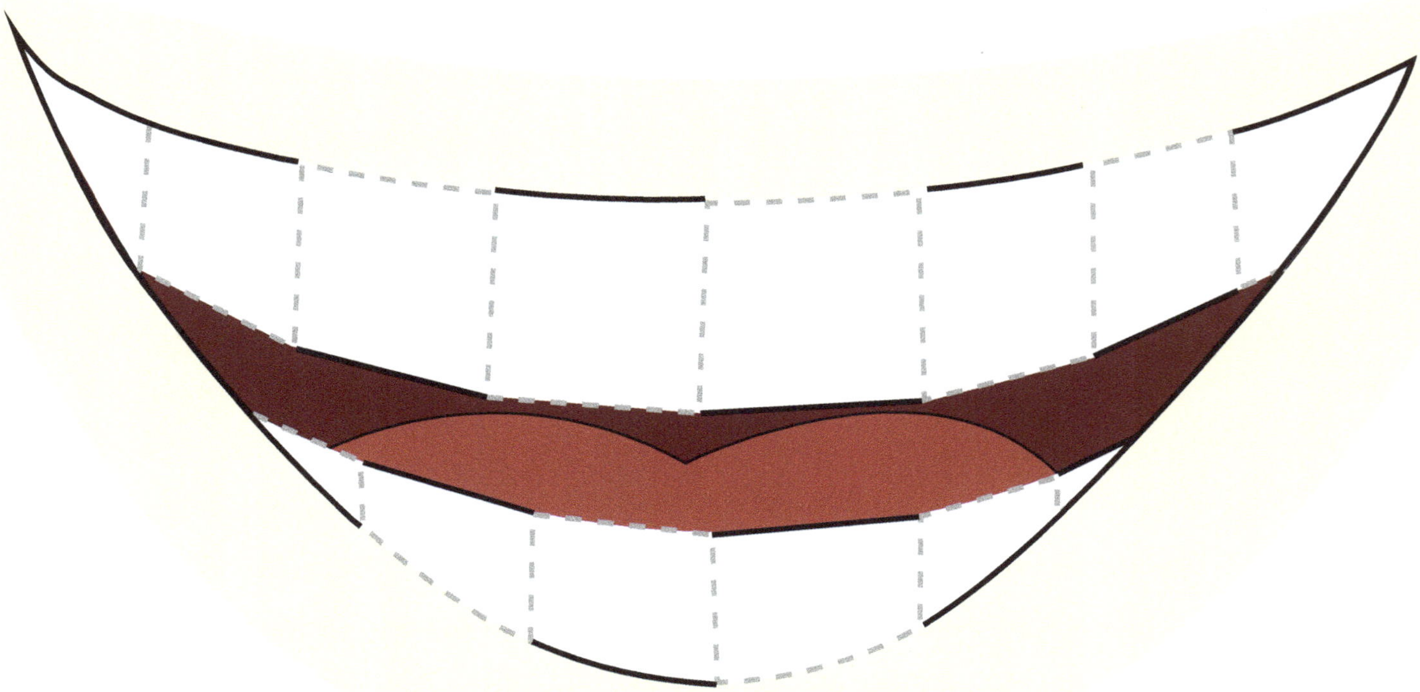

Let's practice the letter "T" now!

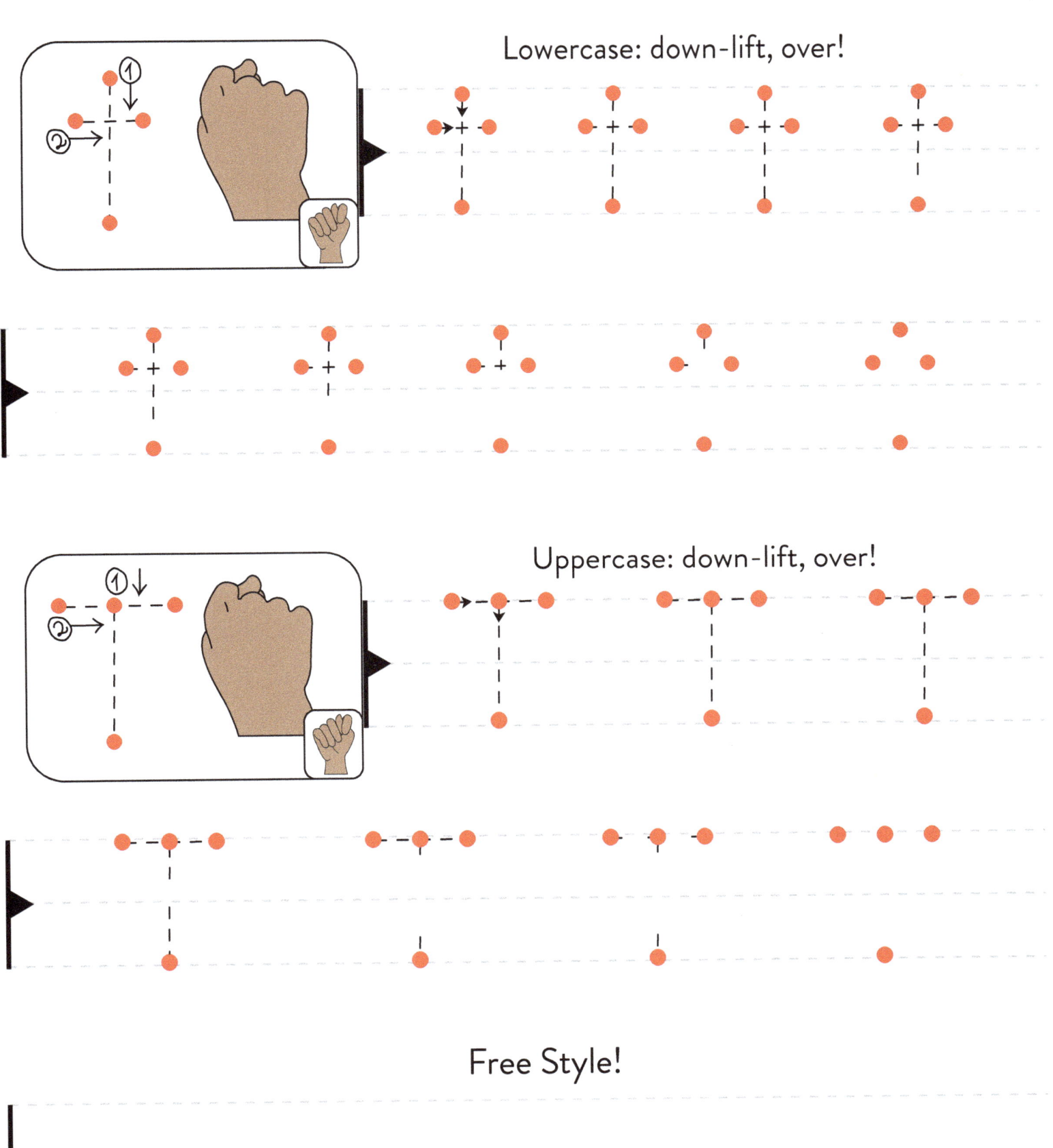

Lowercase: down-lift, over!

Uppercase: down-lift, over!

Free Style!

THIS IS THE LETTER "I": TRACE IT WITH YOUR FINGER

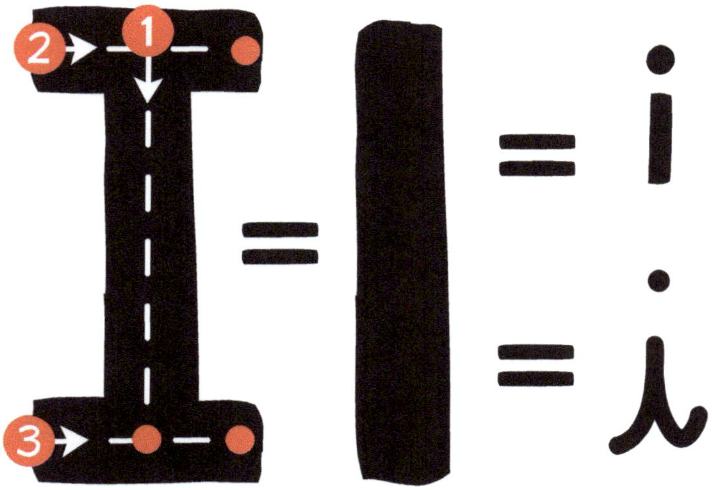

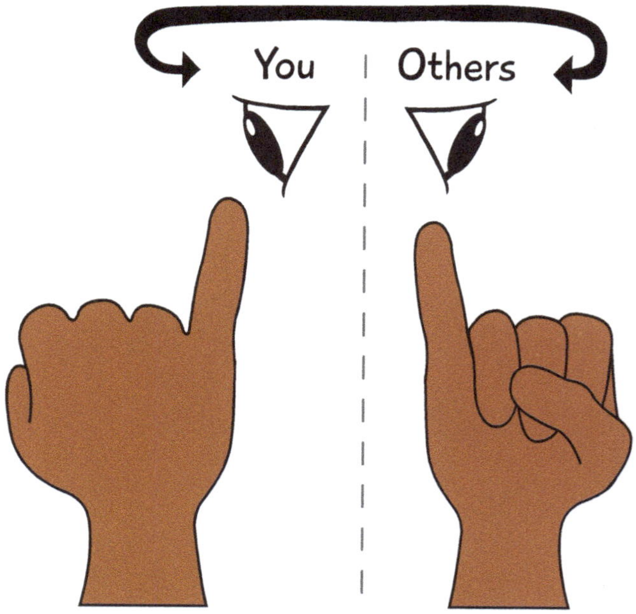

I = I = i
I = I = i

You | Others

Insect

Iguana

Inside

Igloo

Ice

Trace the dotted lines with a pencil or pen to finish the picture!

Let's practice the letter "I" now!

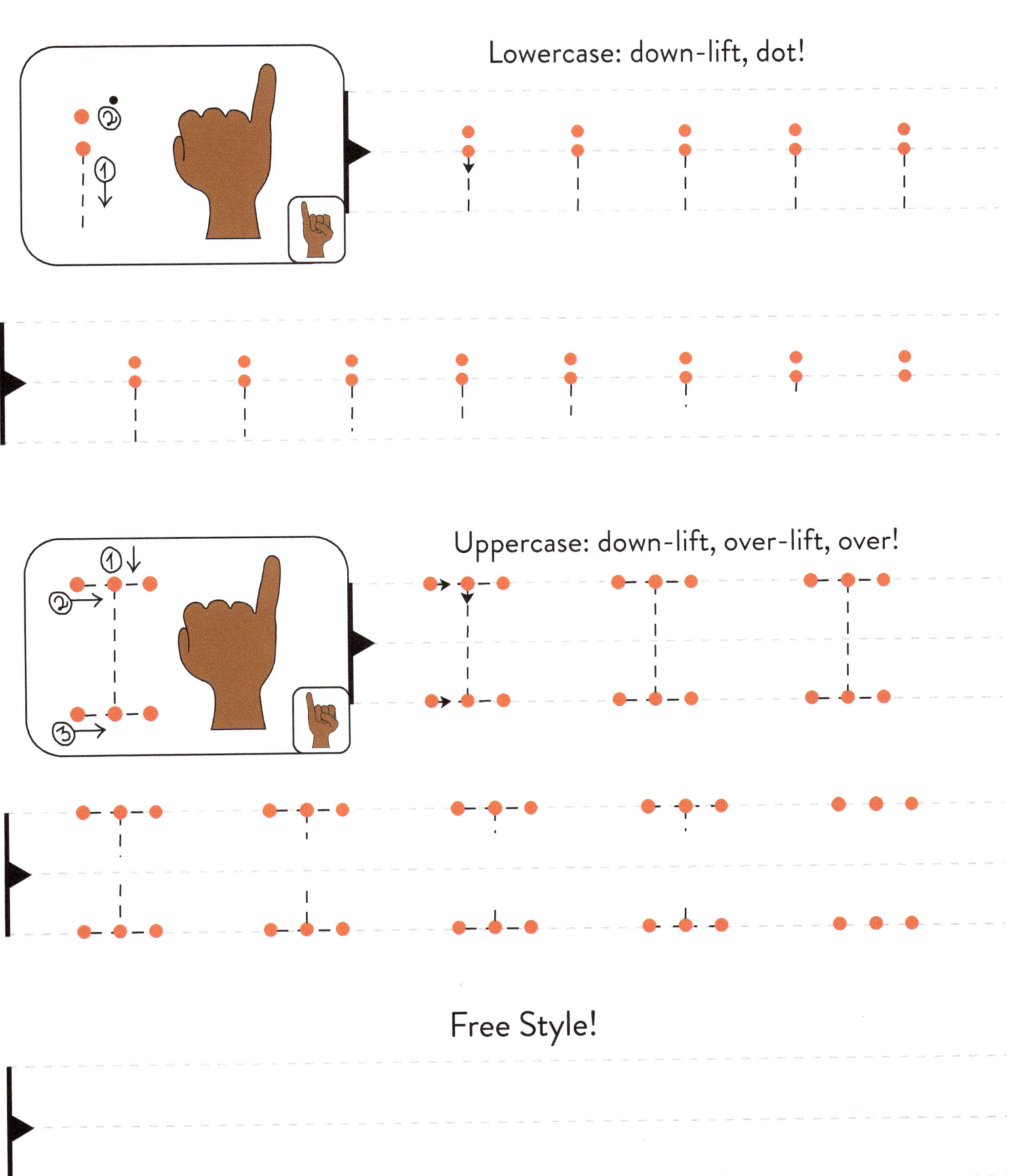

Lowercase: down-lift, dot!

Uppercase: down-lift, over-lift, over!

Free Style!

THIS IS THE LETTER "R": TRACE IT WITH YOUR FINGER

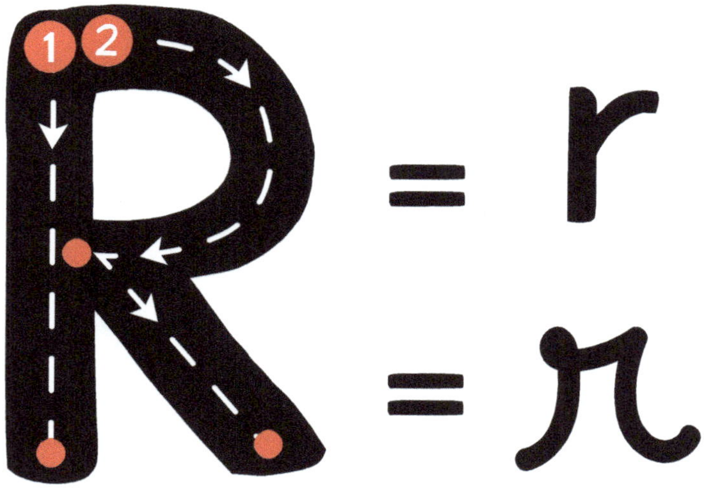

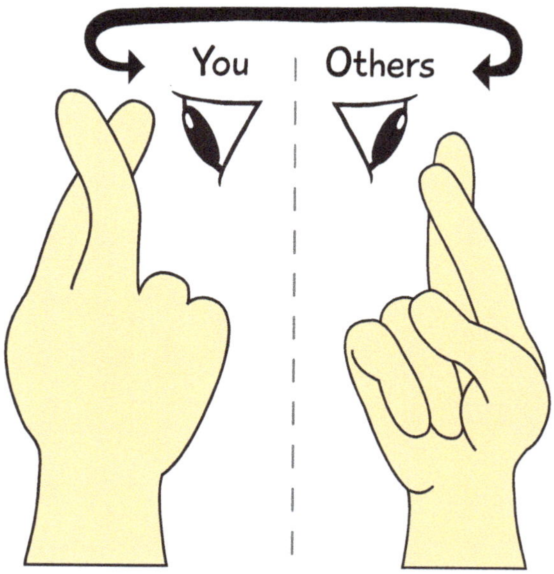

R = r

R = ɾ

You | Others

Rabbit

Robot

Rooster

River

Rice

Trace the dotted lines with a pencil or pen to finish the picture!

Let's practice the letter "R" now!

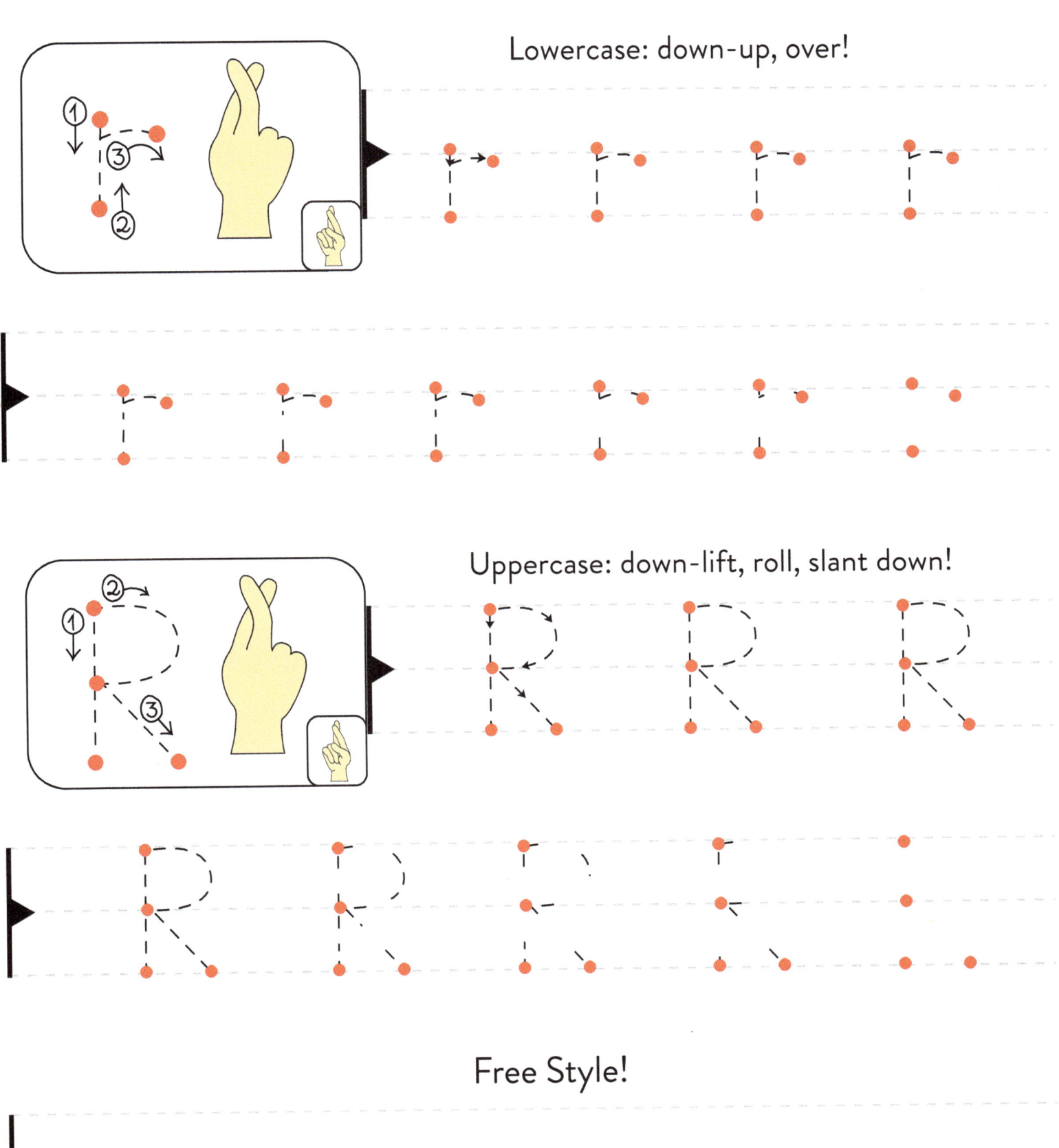

Lowercase: down-up, over!

Uppercase: down-lift, roll, slant down!

Free Style!

THIS IS THE LETTER "N": TRACE IT WITH YOUR FINGER

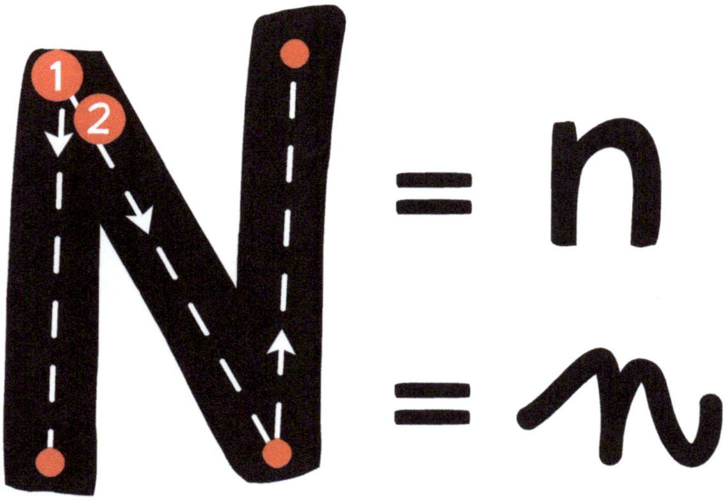

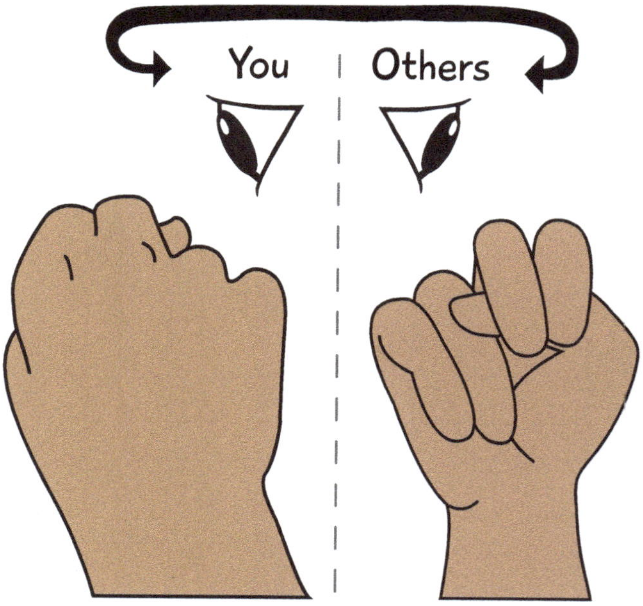

N = n
N = n

You | Others

Ninja   Neck   Napkin

Nest   Nose

Trace the dotted lines with a pencil or pen to finish the picture!

Let's practice the letter "N" now!

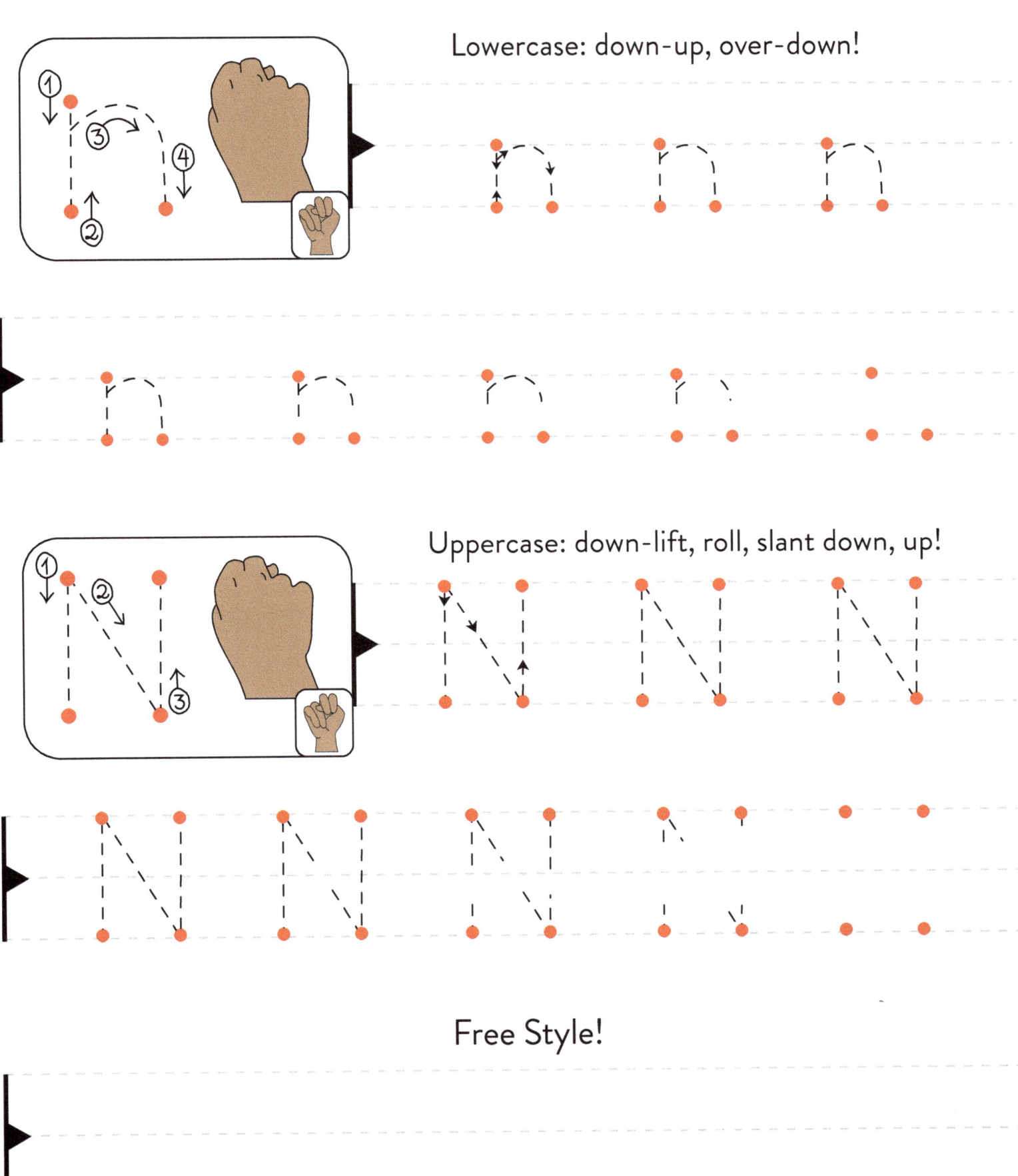

Lowercase: down-up, over-down!

Uppercase: down-lift, roll, slant down, up!

Free Style!

THIS IS THE LETTER "H": TRACE IT WITH YOUR FINGER

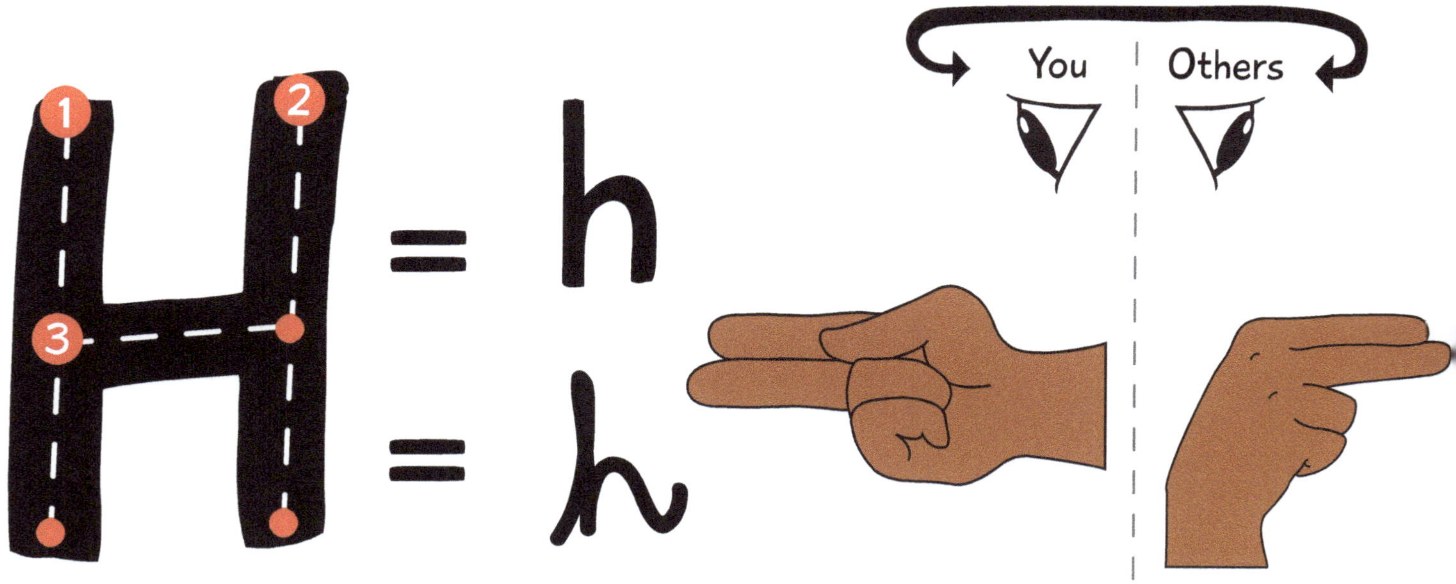

H = h

H = h

You   Others

House

Hammer

Hedgehog

Horse

High

Trace the dotted lines with a pencil or pen to finish the picture!

Let's practice the letter "H" now!

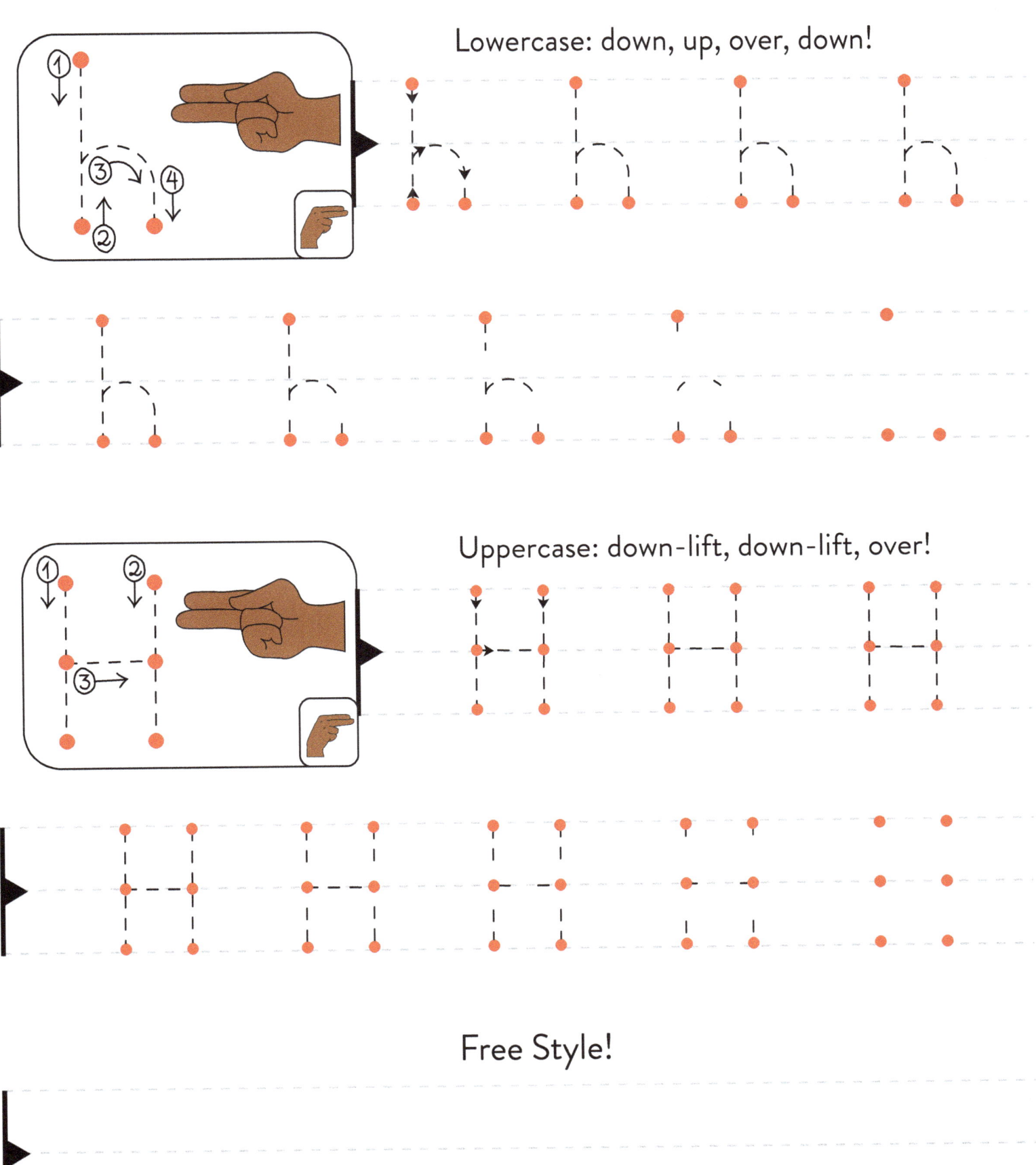

Lowercase: down, up, over, down!

Uppercase: down-lift, down-lift, over!

Free Style!

THIS IS THE LETTER "M": TRACE IT WITH YOUR FINGER

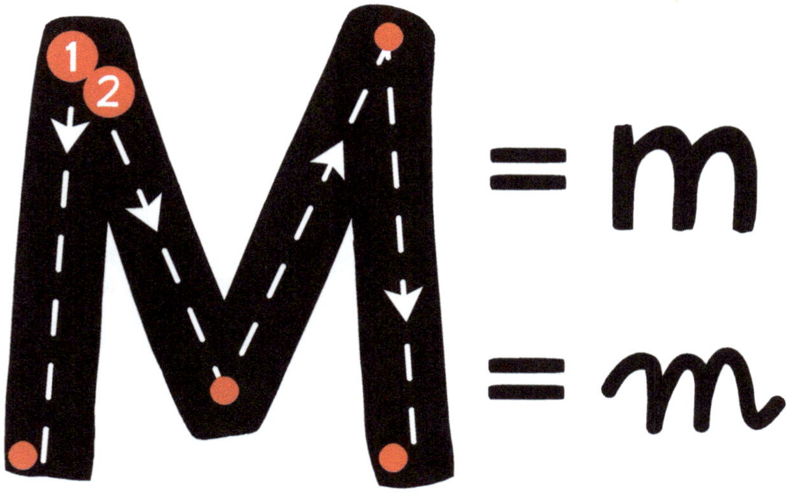

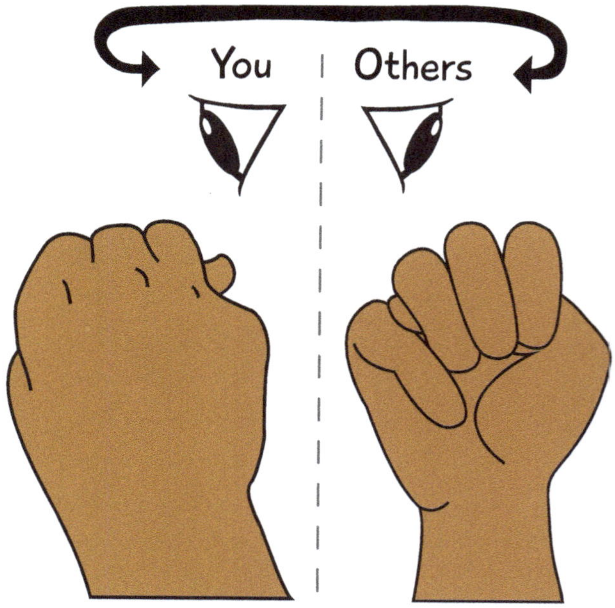

M = m

M = m

You | Others

Milk

Monkey

Mushroom

Mommy

Mask

Trace the dotted lines with a pencil or pen to finish the picture!

Let's practice the letter "M" now!

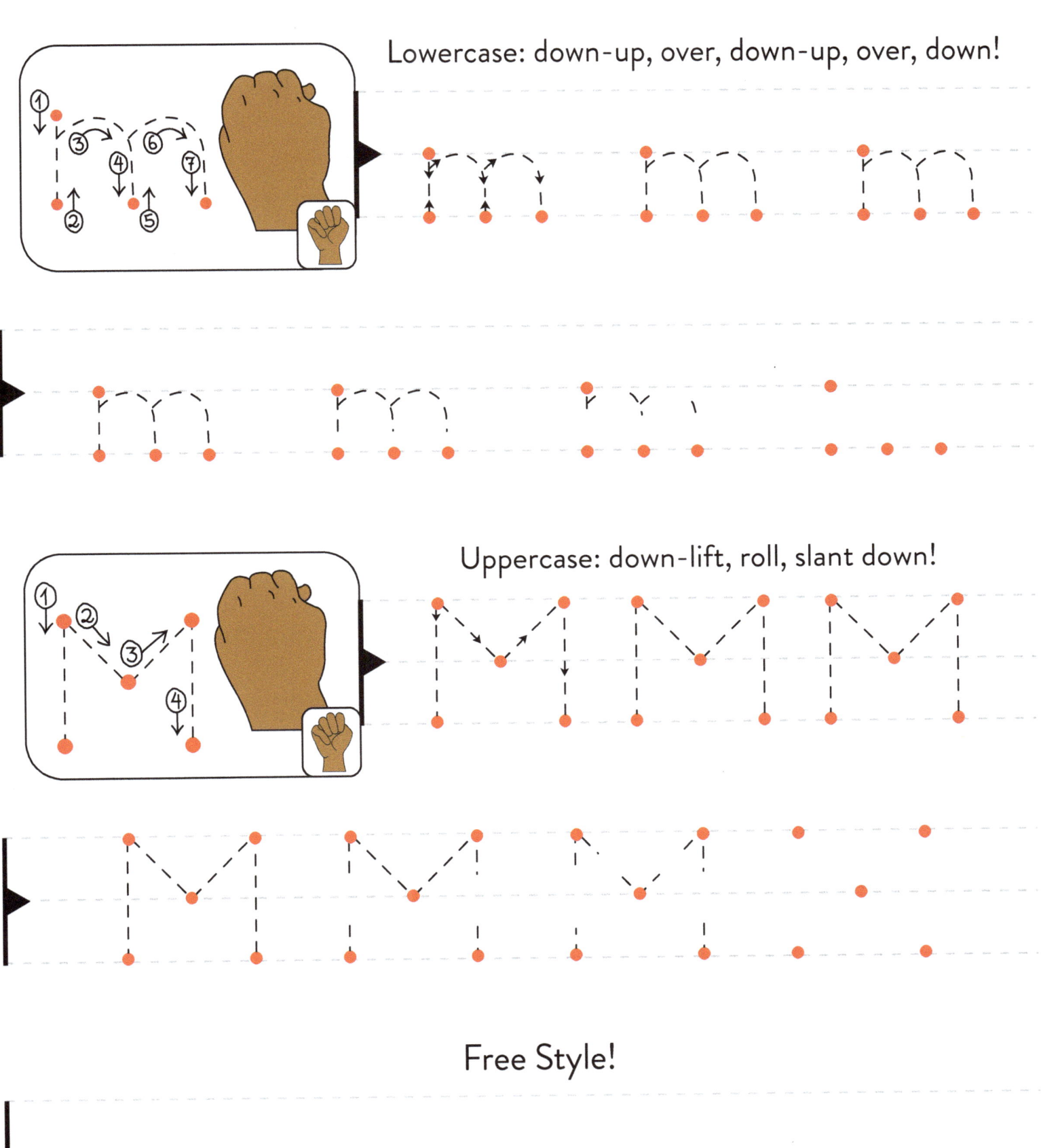

Lowercase: down-up, over, down-up, over, down!

Uppercase: down-lift, roll, slant down!

Free Style!

THIS IS THE LETTER "C": TRACE IT WITH YOUR FINGER

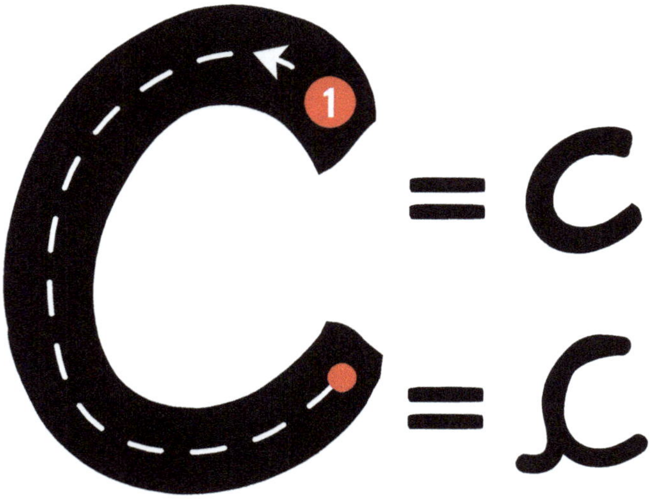

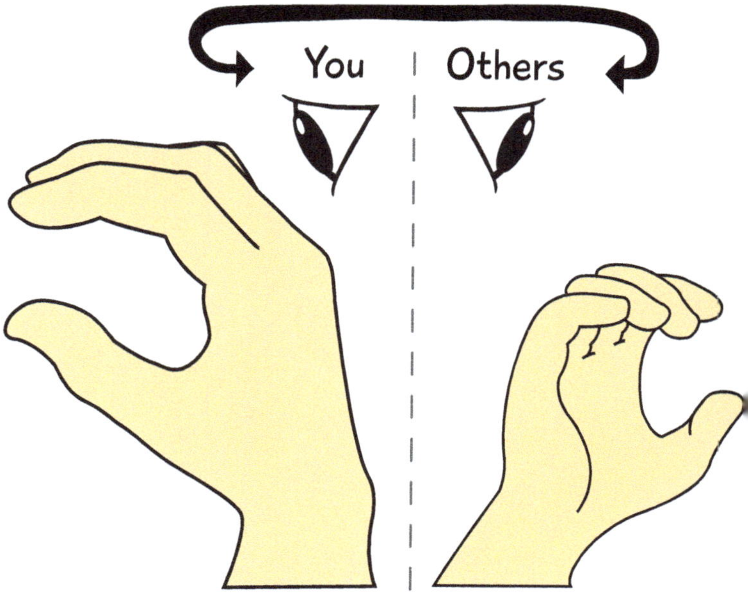

C = c

C = c

You | Others

Cake

Cupcake

Circle

Cloud

Cat

Trace the dotted lines with a pencil or pen to finish the picture!

Let's practice the letter "C" now!

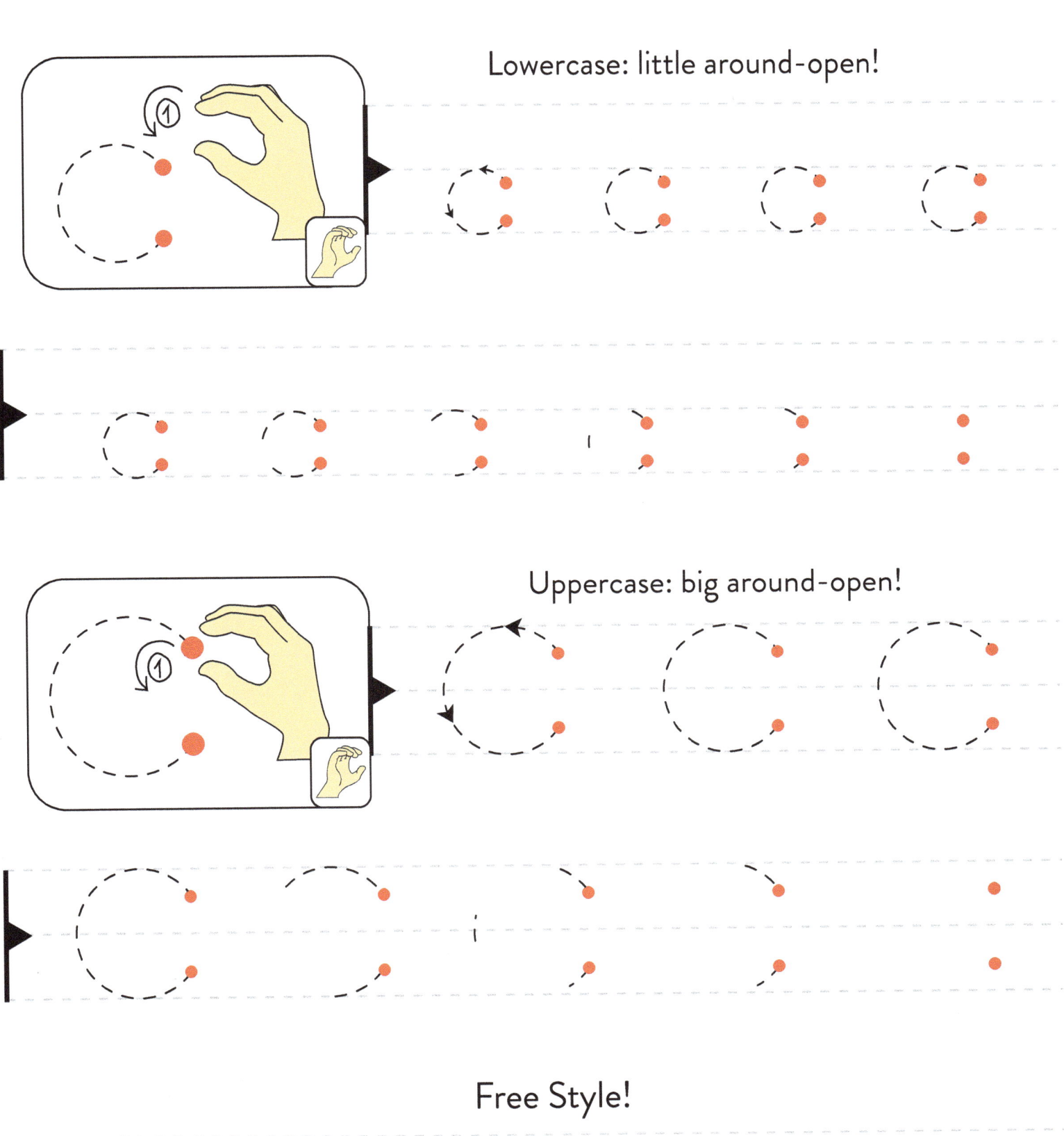

Lowercase: little around-open!

Uppercase: big around-open!

Free Style!

THIS IS THE LETTER "E": TRACE IT WITH YOUR FINGER

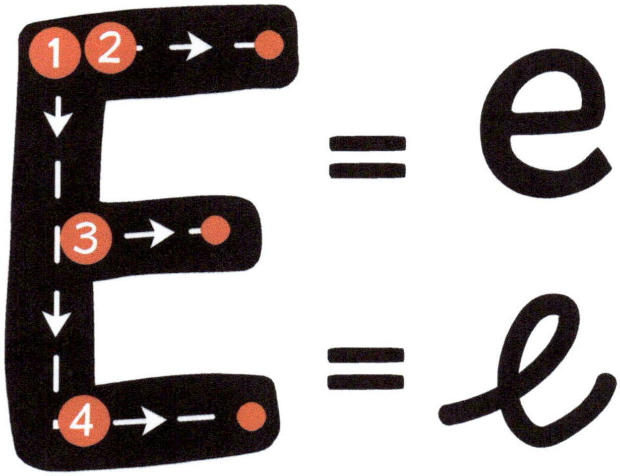

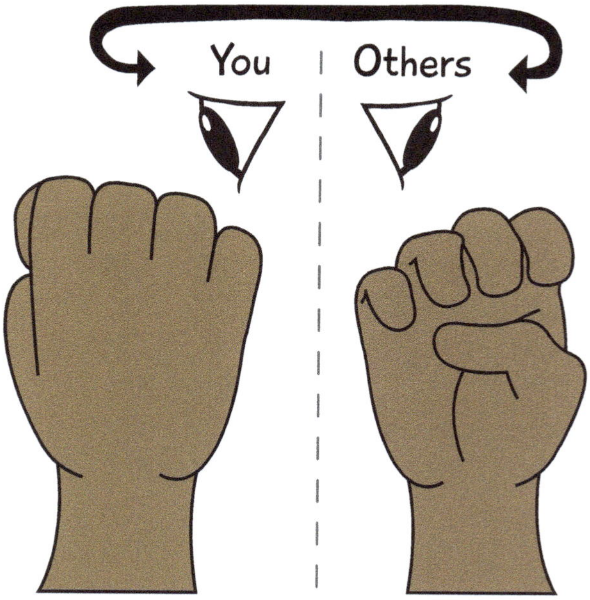

E = e

E = e

You | Others

Earth

Envelope

Elephant

Egg

Elbow

Trace the dotted lines with a pencil or pen to finish the picture!

Let's practice the letter "E" now!

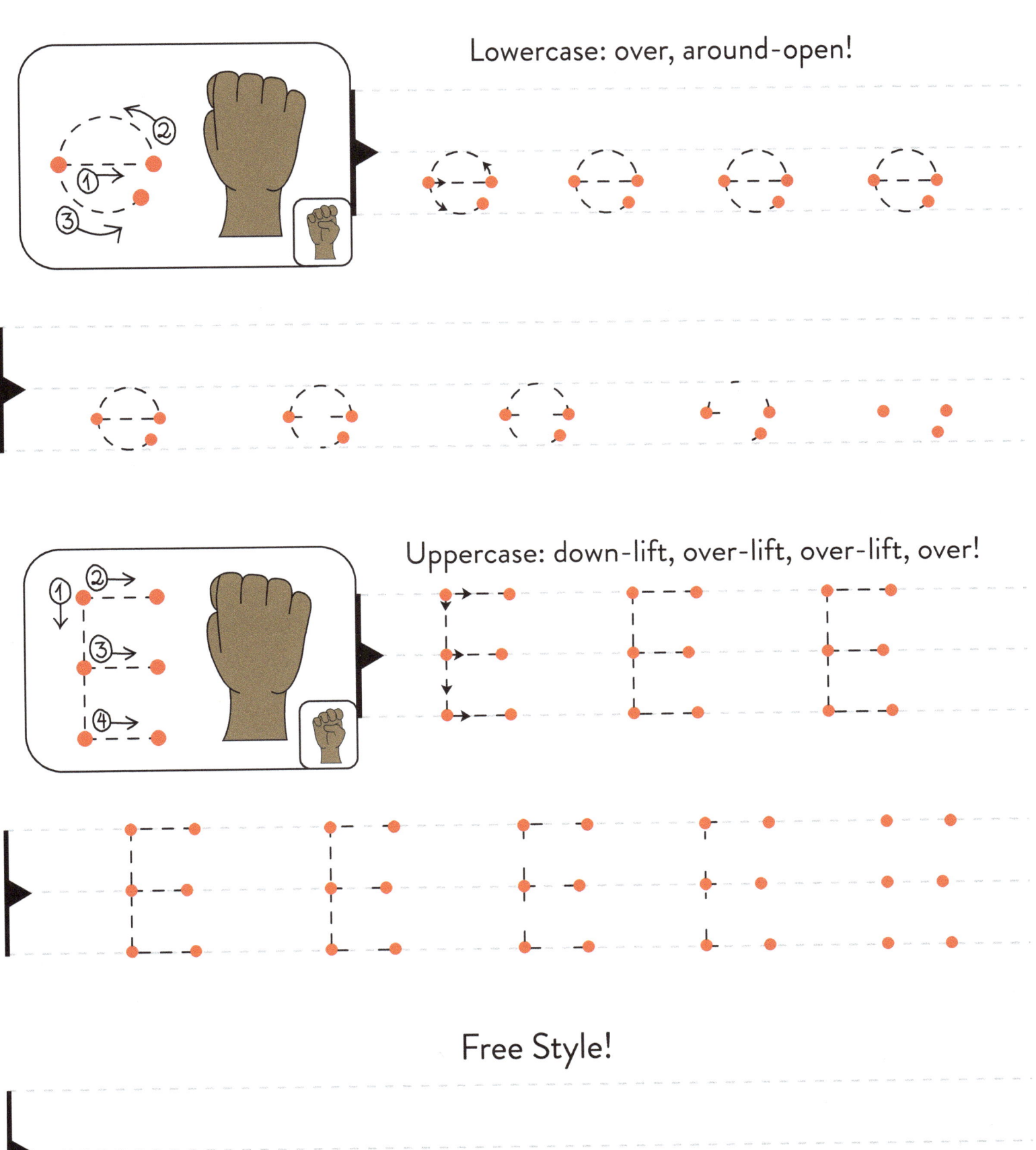

Lowercase: over, around-open!

Uppercase: down-lift, over-lift, over-lift, over!

Free Style!

THIS IS THE LETTER "S": TRACE IT WITH YOUR FINGER

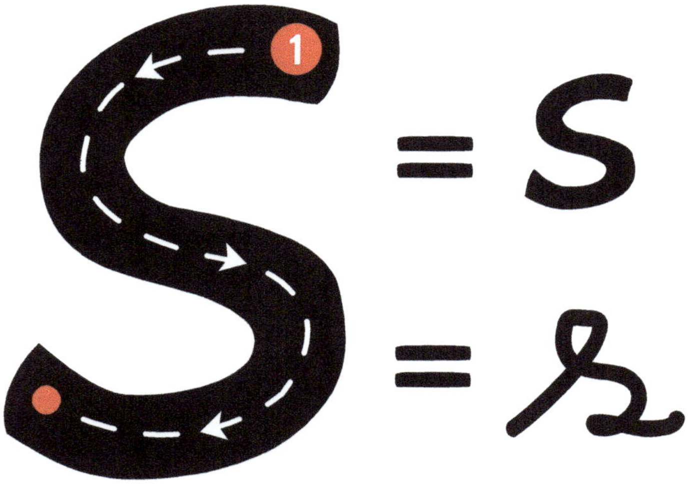

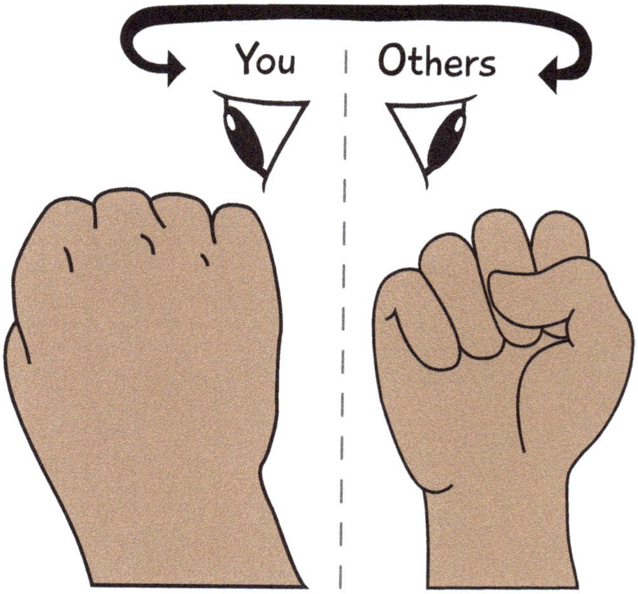

S = S

S = ⟨cursive s⟩

You | Others

Sun
Spiders
Scissors
Snakes
Stars

Trace the dotted lines with a pencil or pen to finish the picture!

Let's practice the letter "S" now!

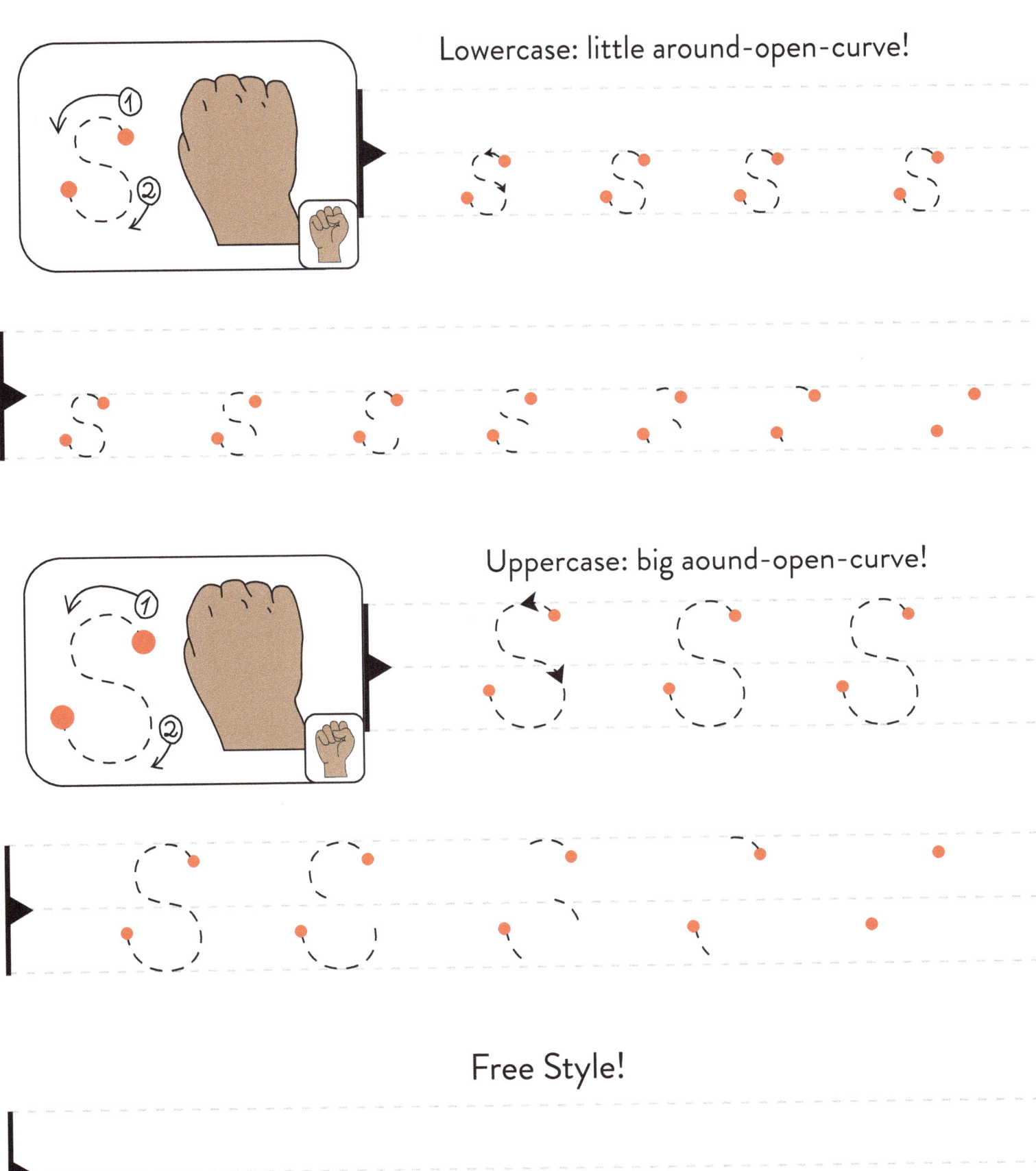

Lowercase: little around-open-curve!

Uppercase: big aound-open-curve!

Free Style!

THIS IS THE LETTER "Q": TRACE IT WITH YOUR FINGER

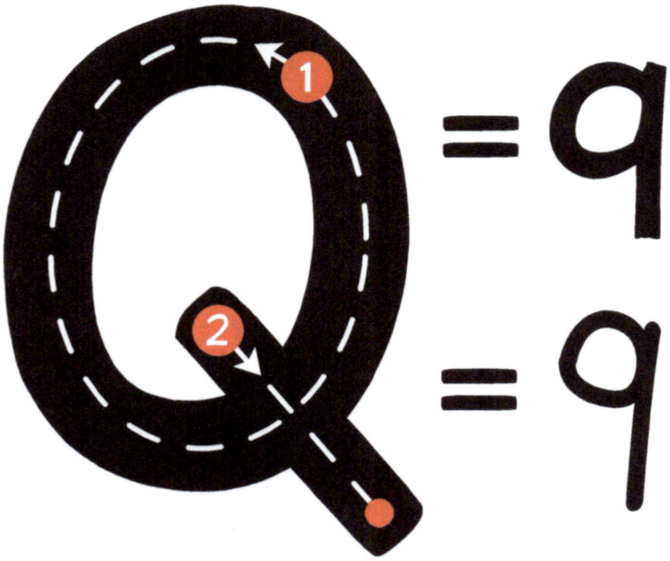

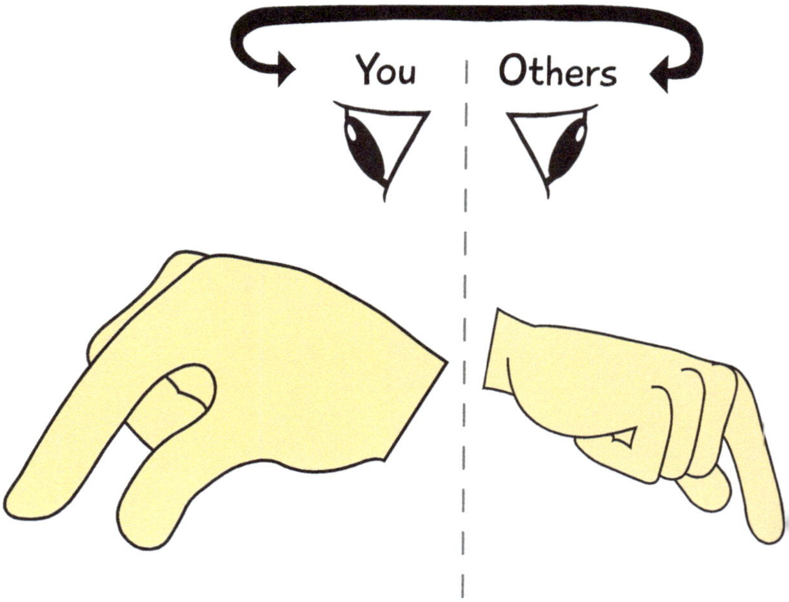

Q = q

Q = q

You | Others

Queen

Quarter

Quicksand

Quiet

Aqua

Trace the dotted lines with a pencil or pen to finish the picture!

Let's practice the letter "Q" now!

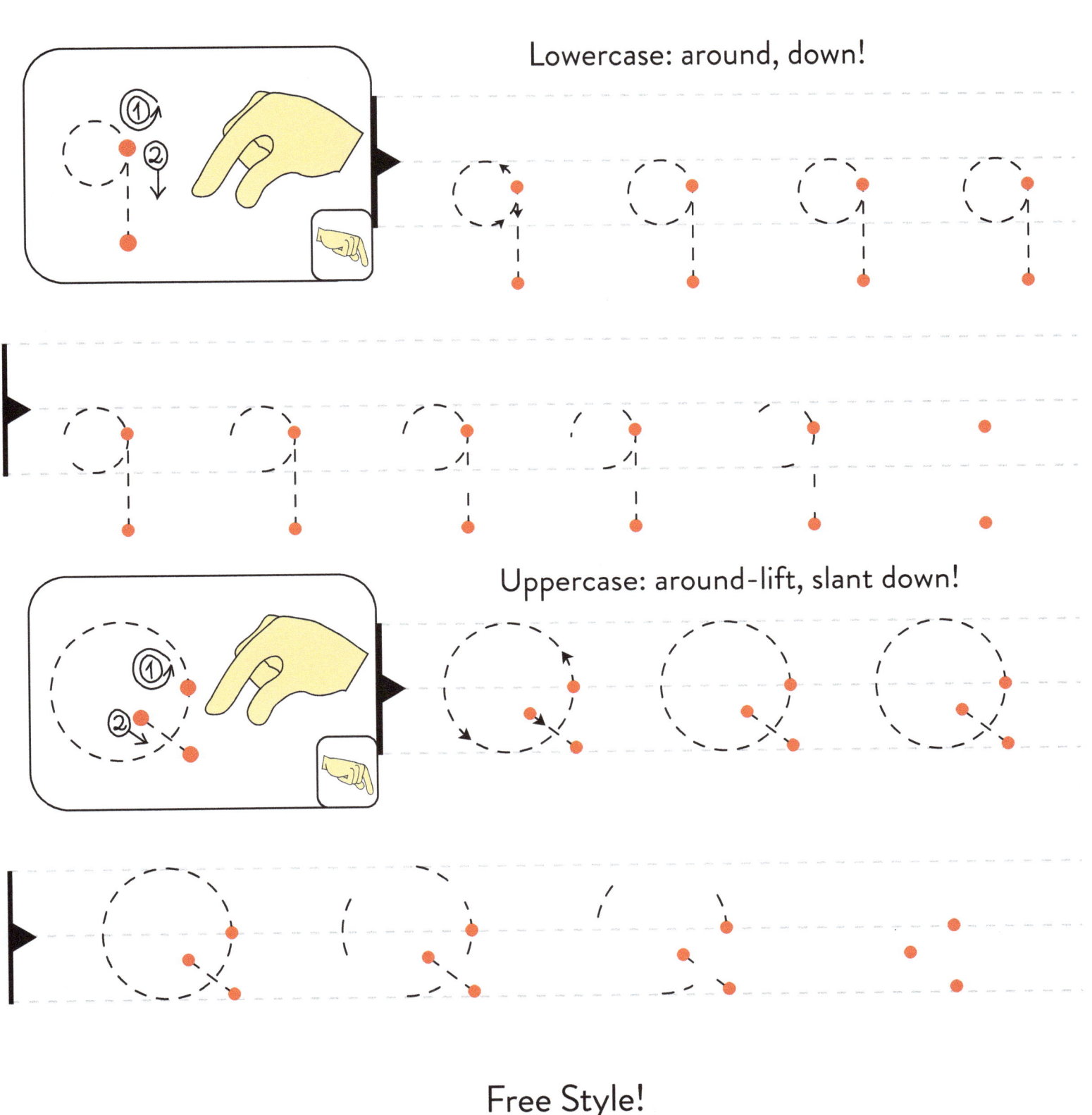

Lowercase: around, down!

Uppercase: around-lift, slant down!

Free Style!

THIS IS THE LETTER "F": TRACE IT WITH YOUR FINGER

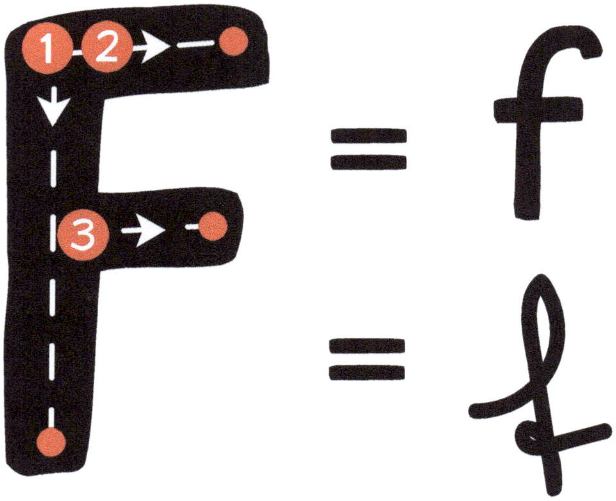

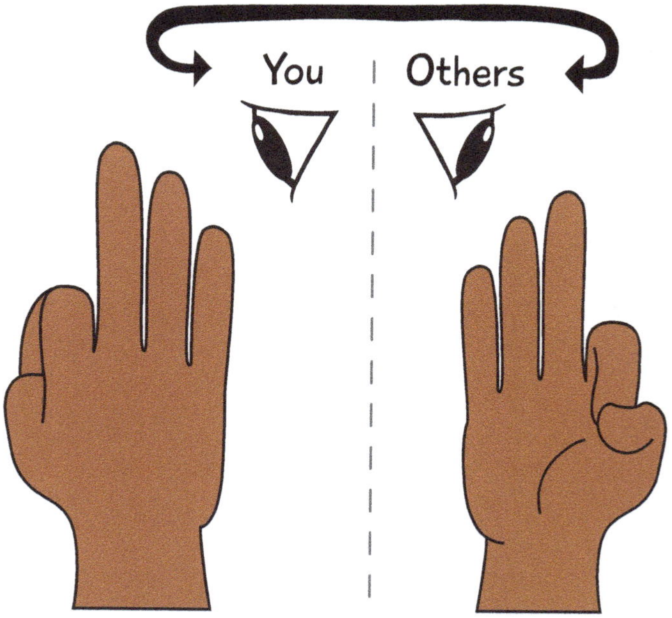

F = f

F = f

You | Others

Fork

Fifteen

Flamingo

Fish

Frog

Trace the dotted lines with a pencil or pen to finish the picture!

Let's practice the letter "F" now!

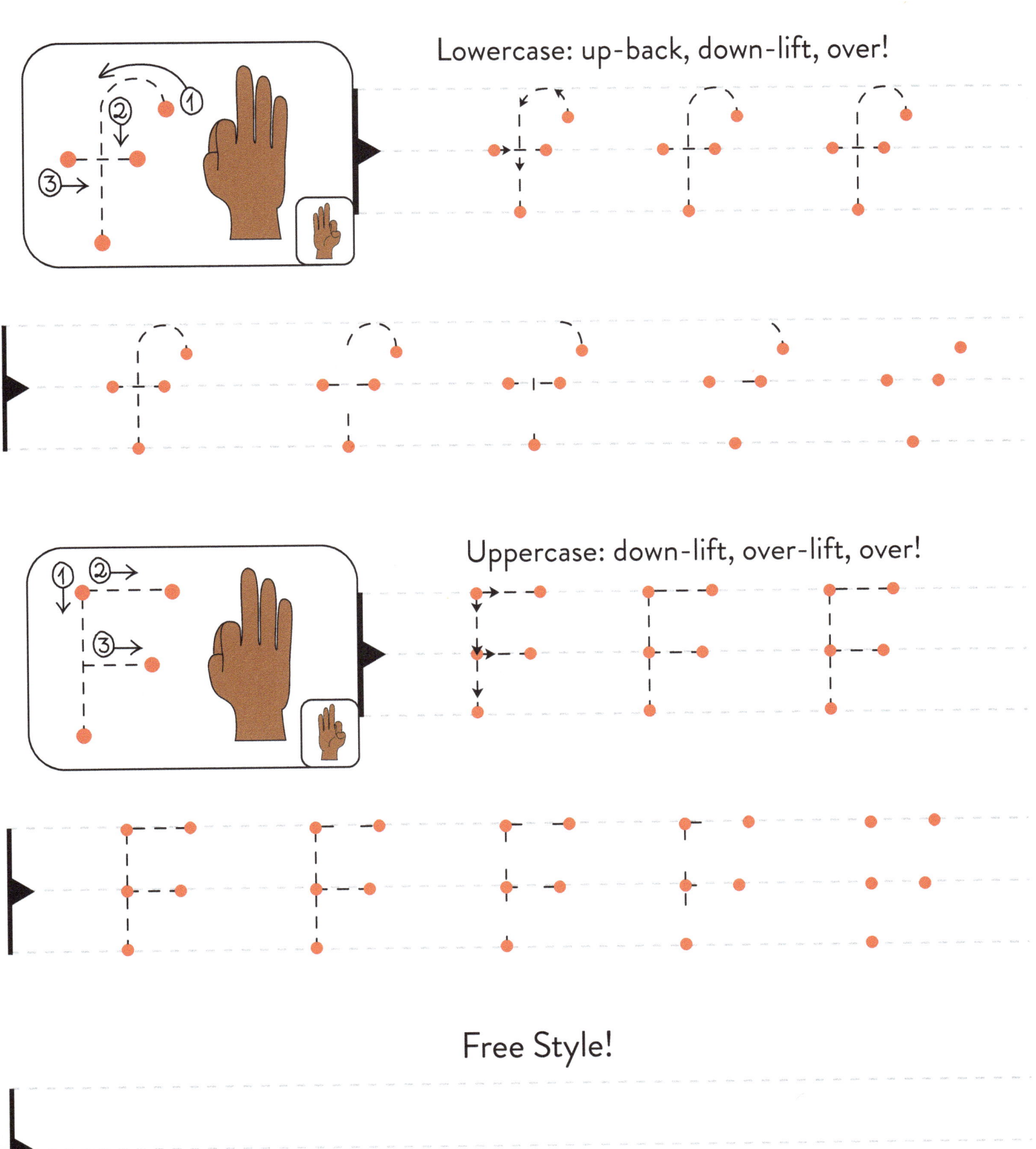

Lowercase: up-back, down-lift, over!

Uppercase: down-lift, over-lift, over!

Free Style!

THIS IS THE LETTER "D": TRACE IT WITH YOUR FINGER

1

2

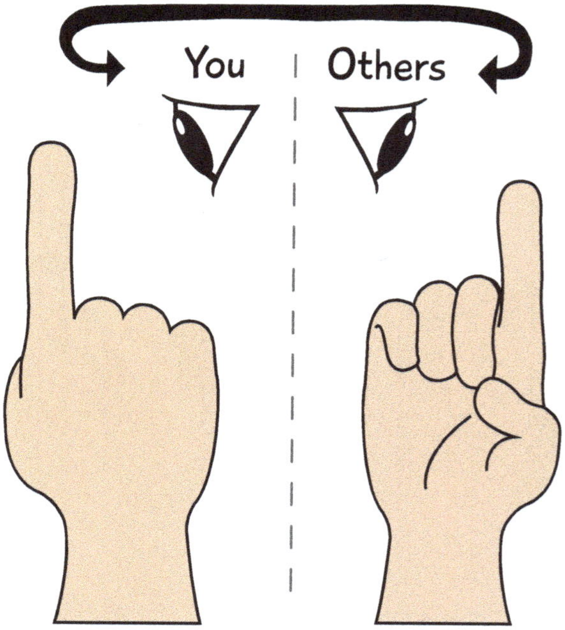

D = d

= d

You | Others

Dragon

Dinosaur

Diamond

Dog

Doctor

Trace the dotted lines with a pencil or pen to finish the picture!

Let's practice the letter "D" now!

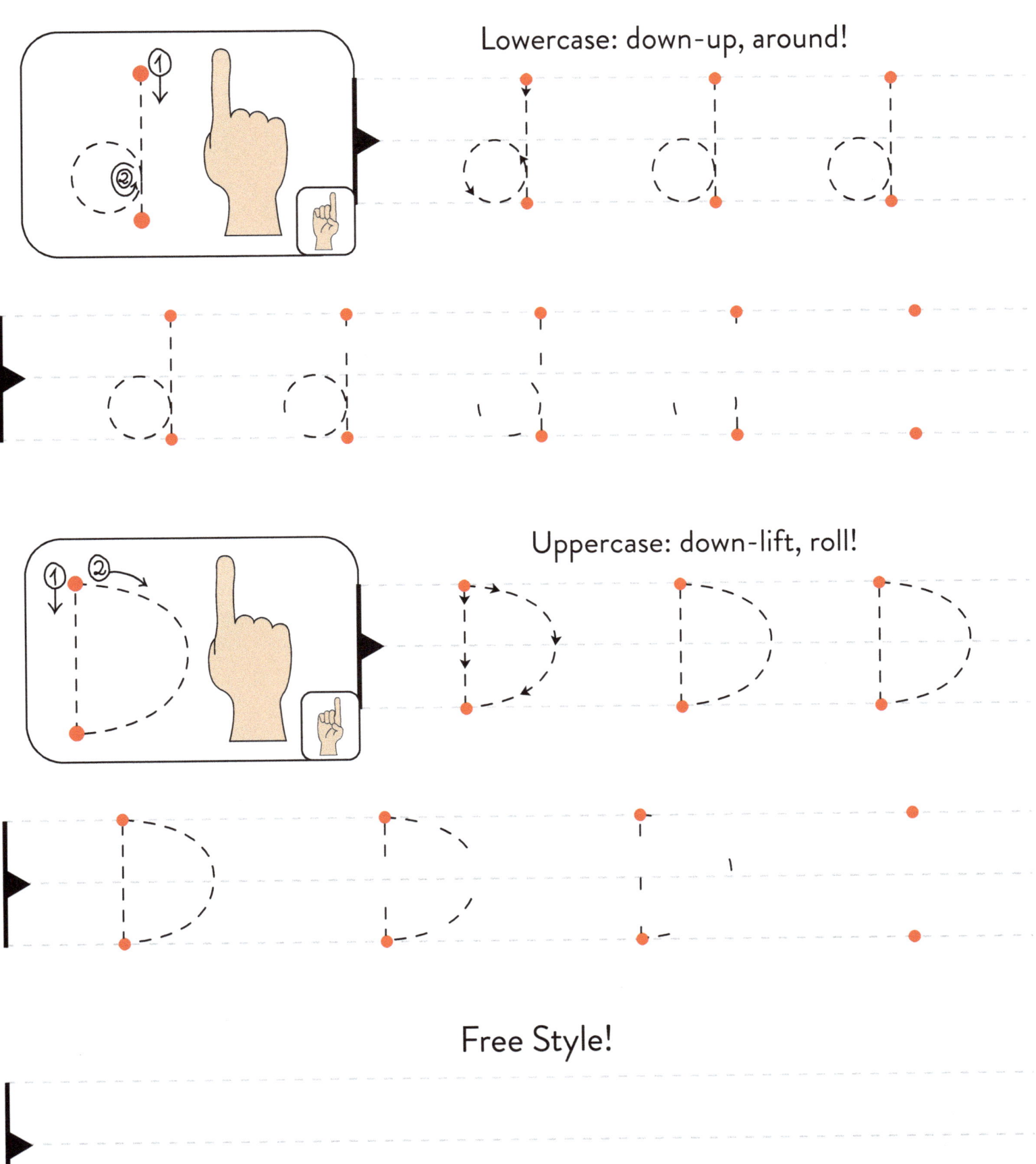

Lowercase: down-up, around!

Uppercase: down-lift, roll!

Free Style!

THIS IS THE LETTER "U": TRACE IT WITH YOUR FINGER

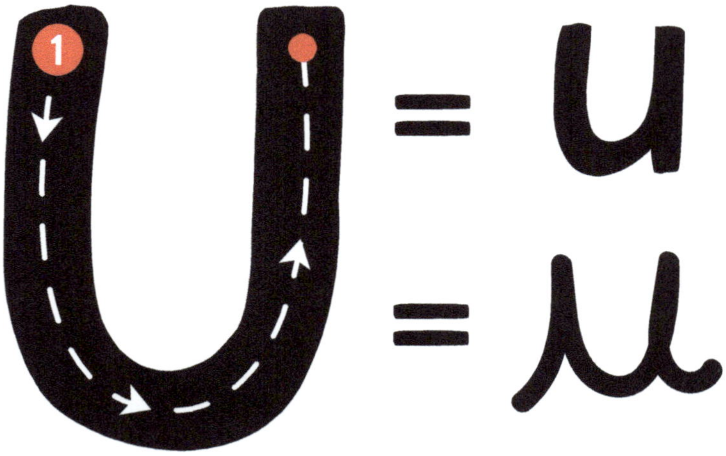

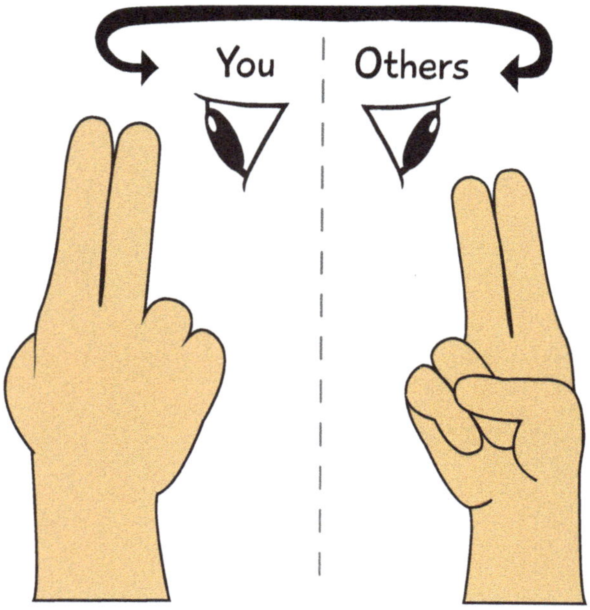

U = u
U = μ

You | Others

Upset
Unicorn
Umbrella
Unique
Uniform

Trace the dotted lines with a pencil or pen to finish the picture!

Let's practice the letter "U" now!

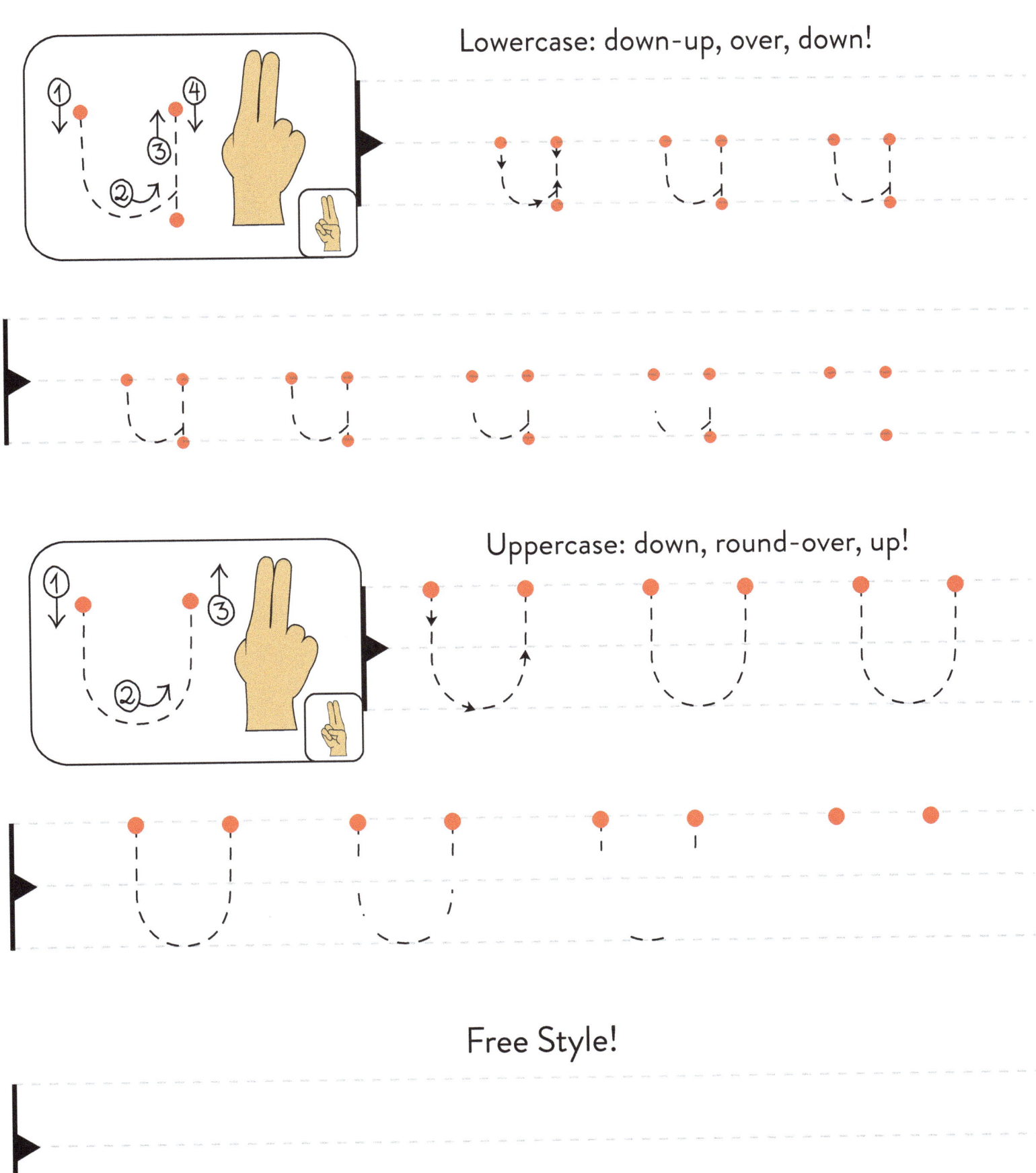

Lowercase: down-up, over, down!

Uppercase: down, round-over, up!

Free Style!

THIS IS THE LETTER "J": TRACE IT WITH YOUR FINGER

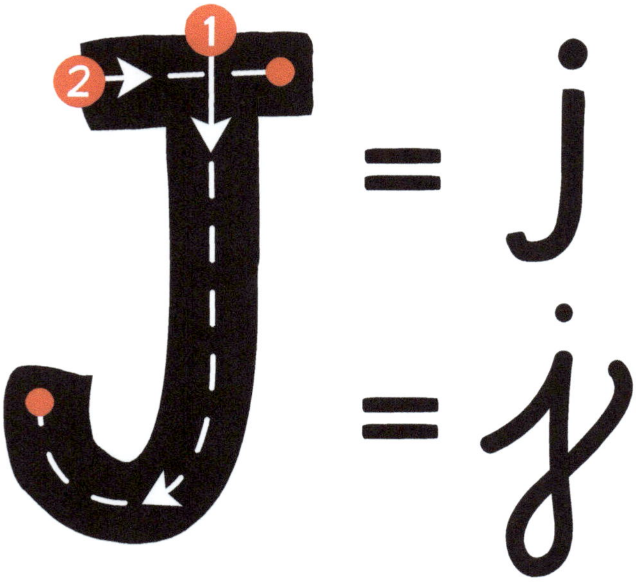

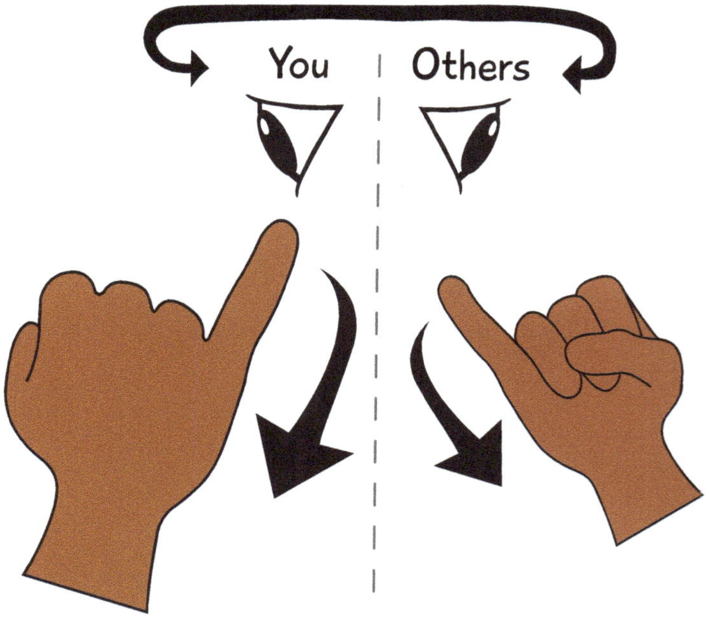

J = j
= *j*

You | Others

January   Jiujitsu   Juice

Jellyfish   Jacket

Trace the dotted lines with a pencil or pen to finish the picture!

Let's practice the letter "J" now!

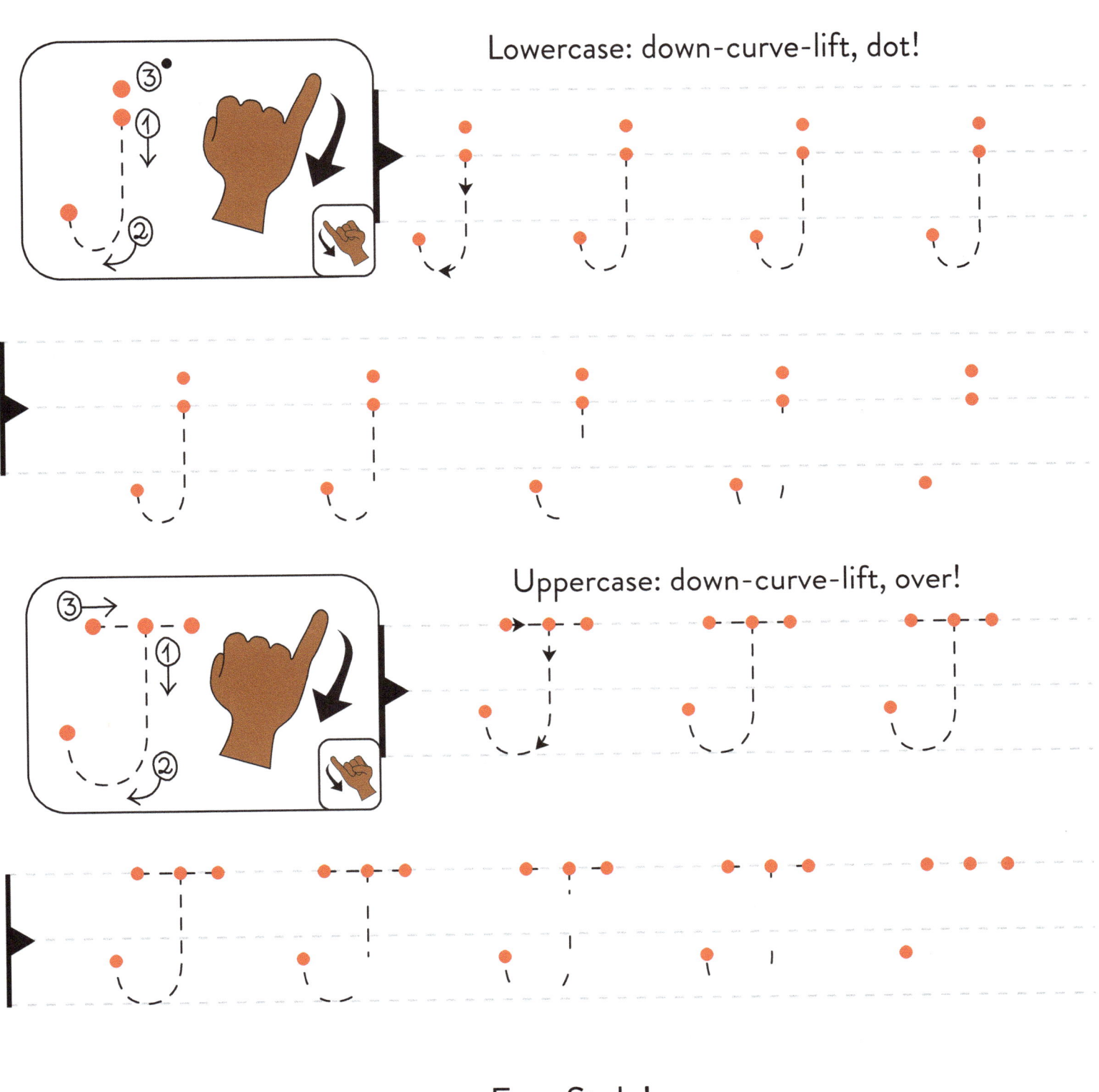

Lowercase: down-curve-lift, dot!

Uppercase: down-curve-lift, over!

Free Style!

THIS IS THE LETTER "G": TRACE IT WITH YOUR FINGER

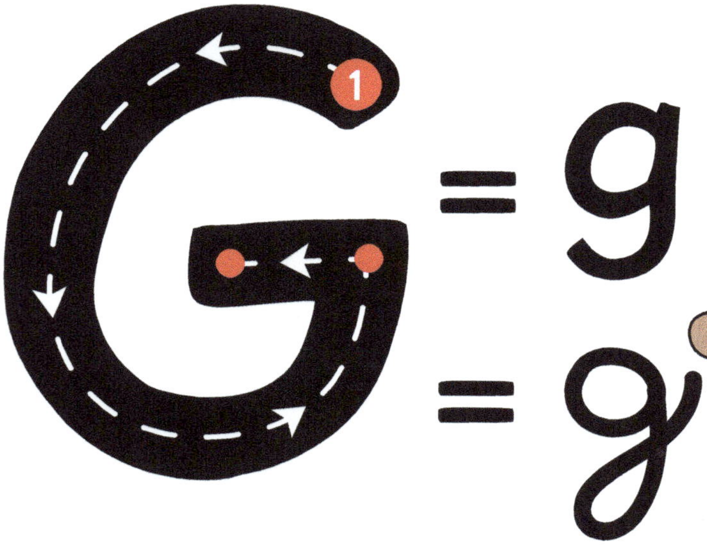

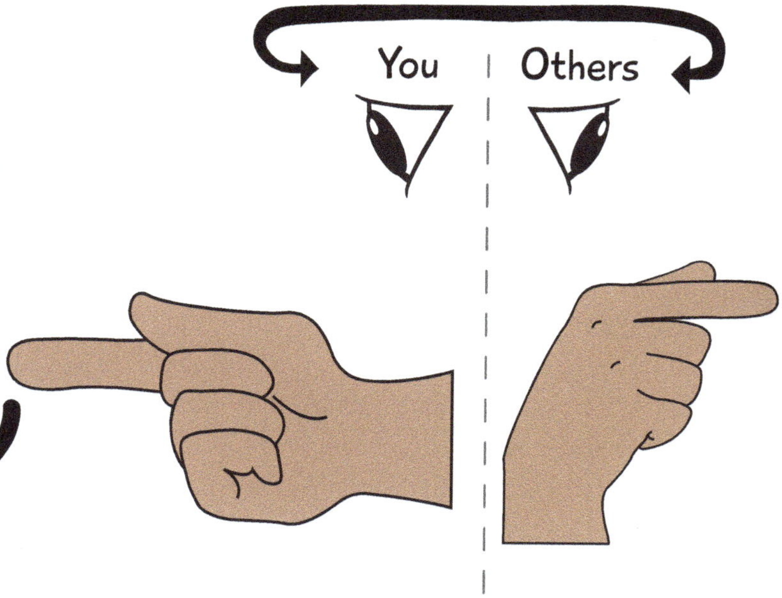

G = g
G = g

You | Others

Gorilla   Ginger   Grapes

Giraffe   Grass

Trace the dotted lines with a pencil or pen to finish the picture!

Let's practice the letter "G" now!

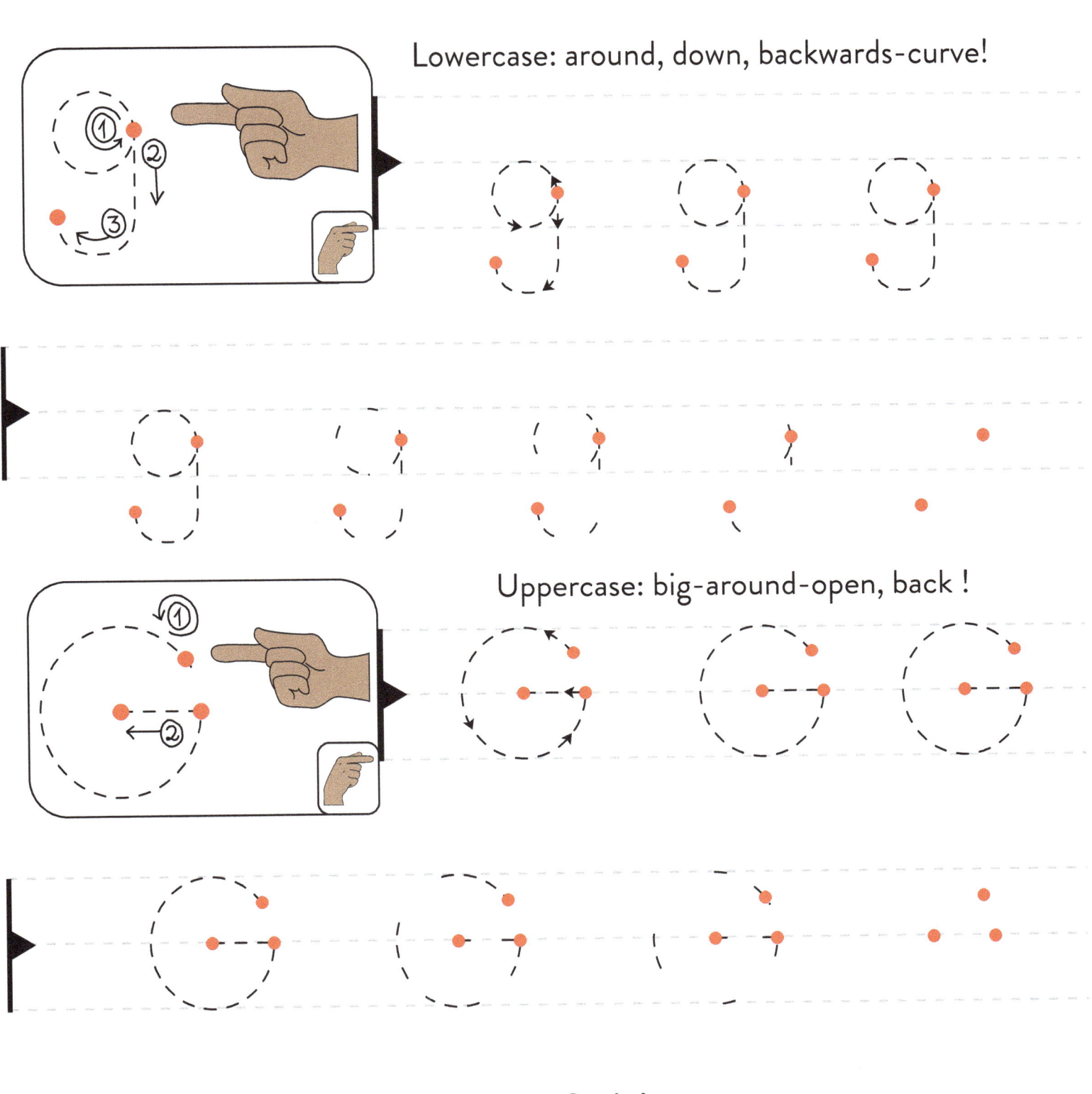

Lowercase: around, down, backwards-curve!

Uppercase: big-around-open, back !

Free Style!

THIS IS THE LETTER "P": TRACE IT WITH YOUR FINGER

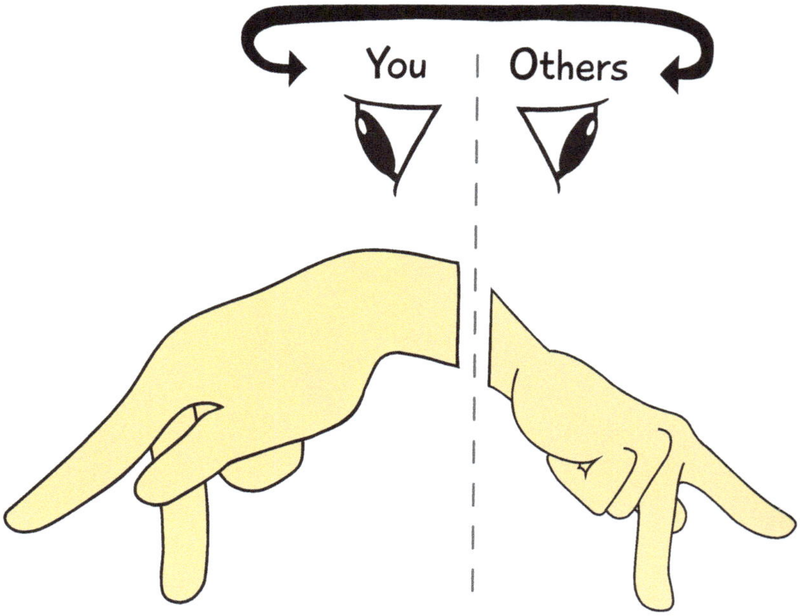

P = p

P = p

You | Others

Pirate

Pumpkin

Pencil

Puppy

Penguin

Trace the dotted lines with a pencil or pen to finish the picture!

Let's practice the letter "P" now!

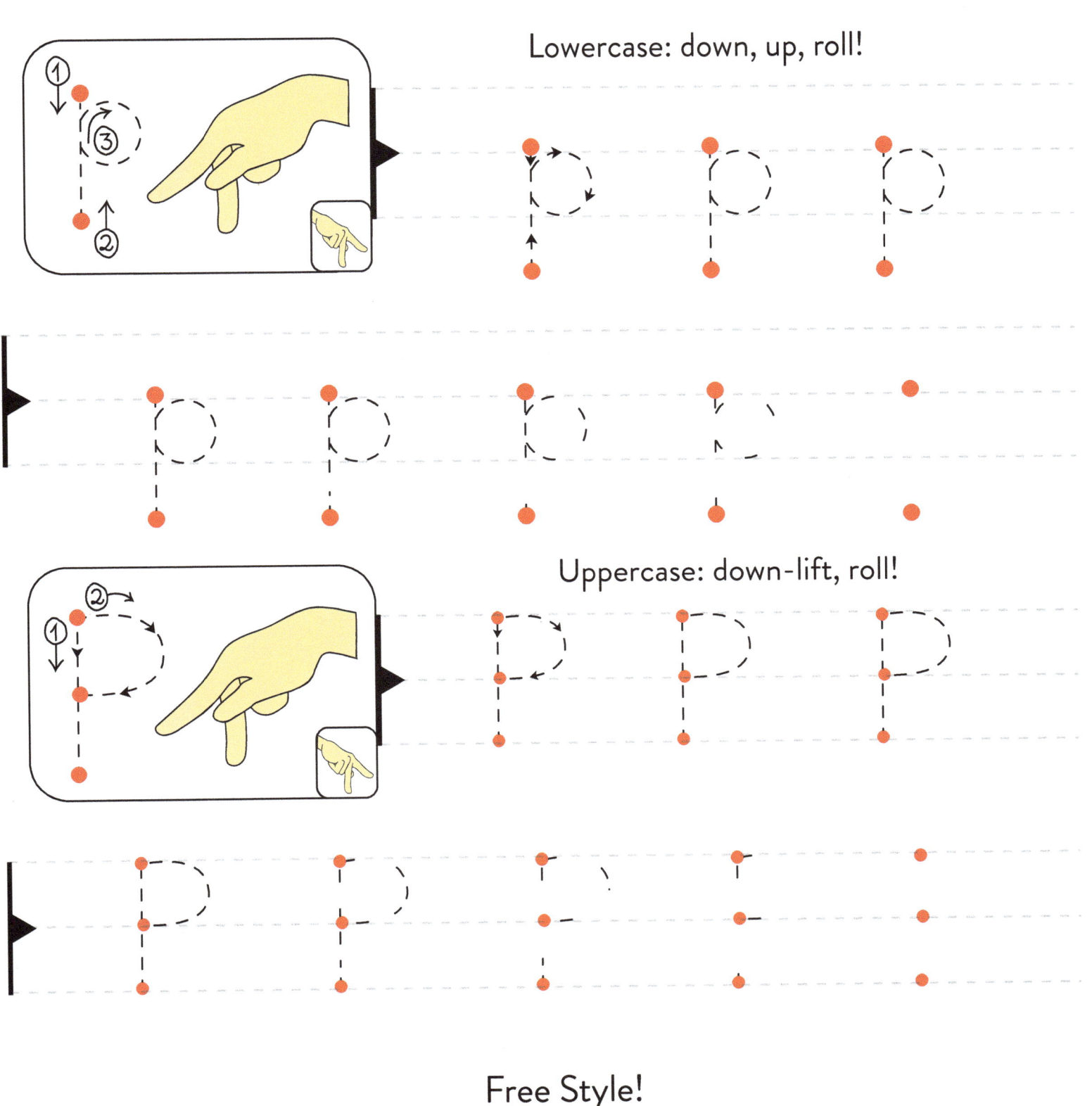

Lowercase: down, up, roll!

Uppercase: down-lift, roll!

Free Style!

THIS IS THE LETTER "B": TRACE IT WITH YOUR FINGER

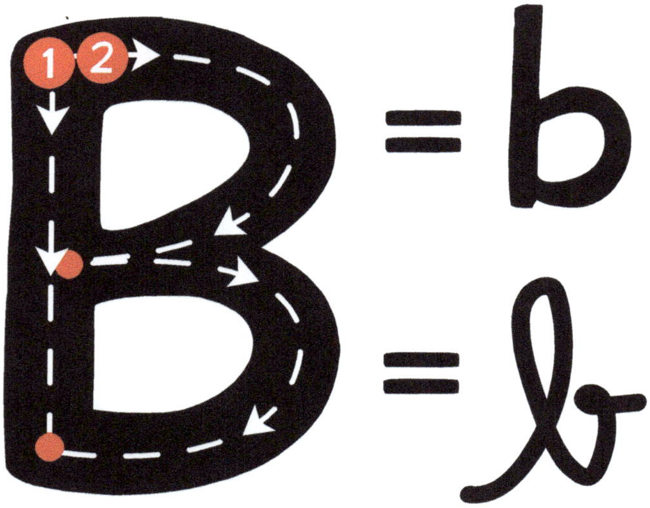

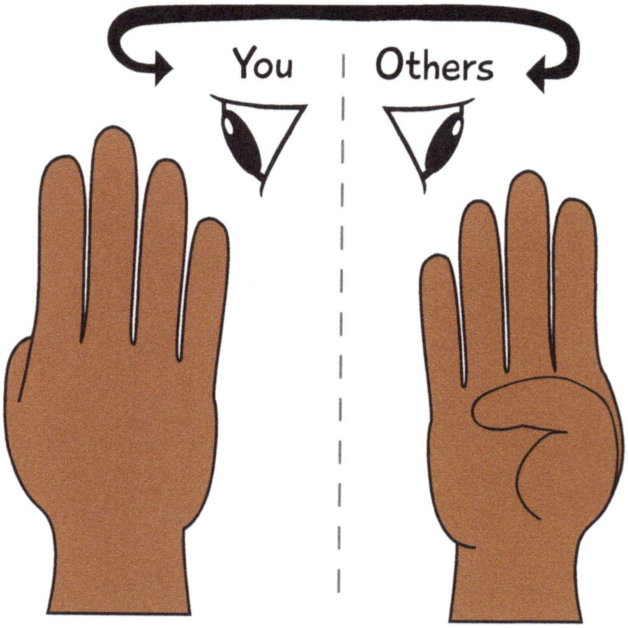

B = b

B = b

1 2

You | Others

Baby **B**ubble **B**arn

Book **B**anana

Trace the dotted lines with a pencil or pen to finish the picture!

Let's practice the letter "B" now!

Lowercase: down, up, roll!

Uppercase: down-lift, roll, roll!

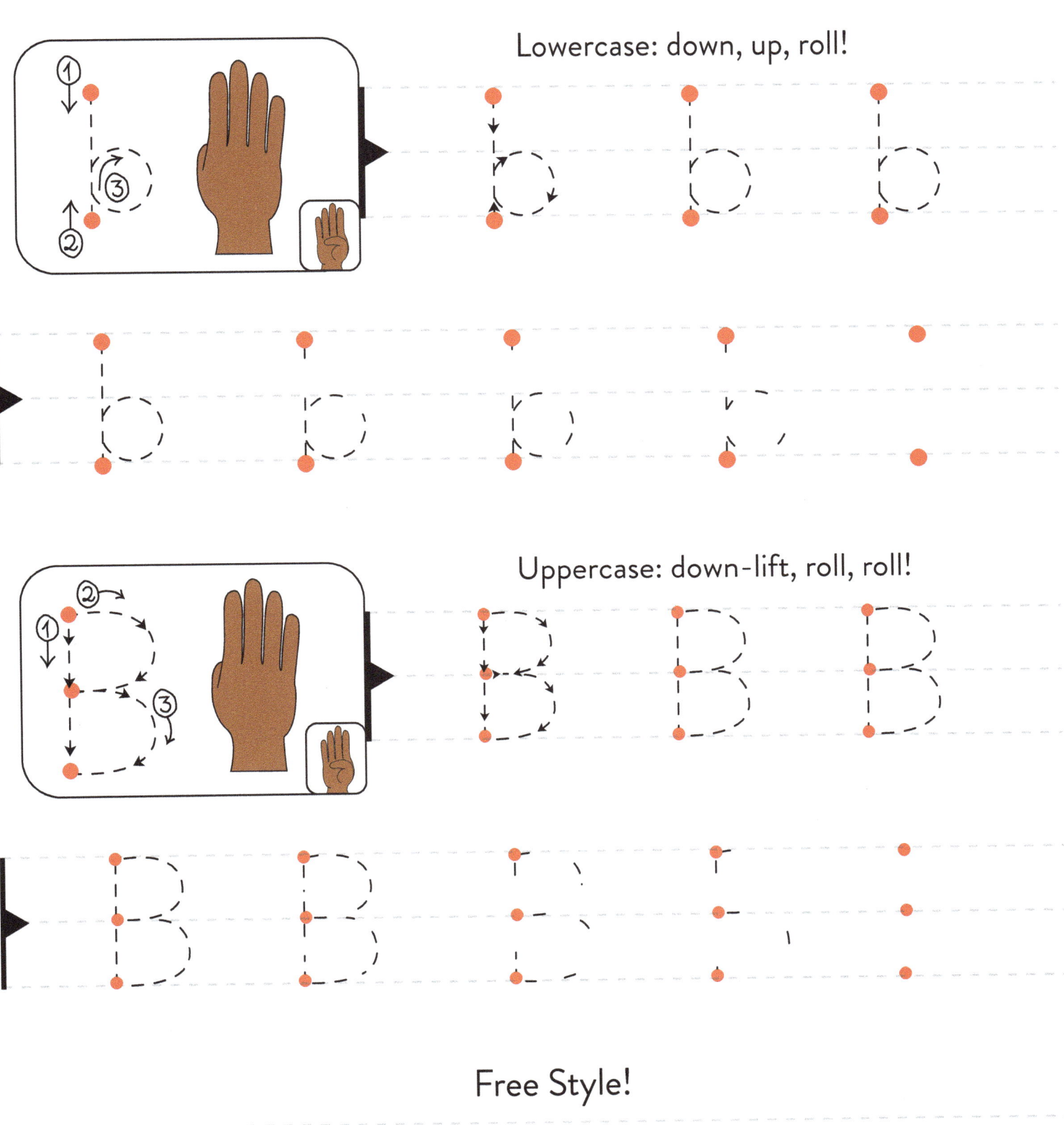

Free Style!

THIS IS THE LETTER "V": TRACE IT WITH YOUR FINGER

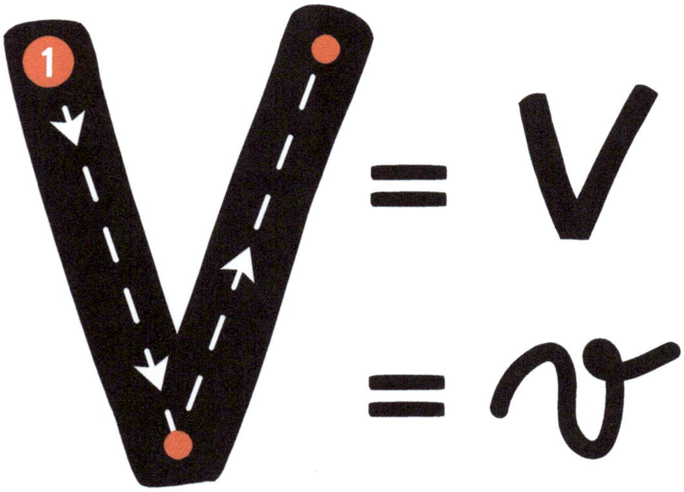

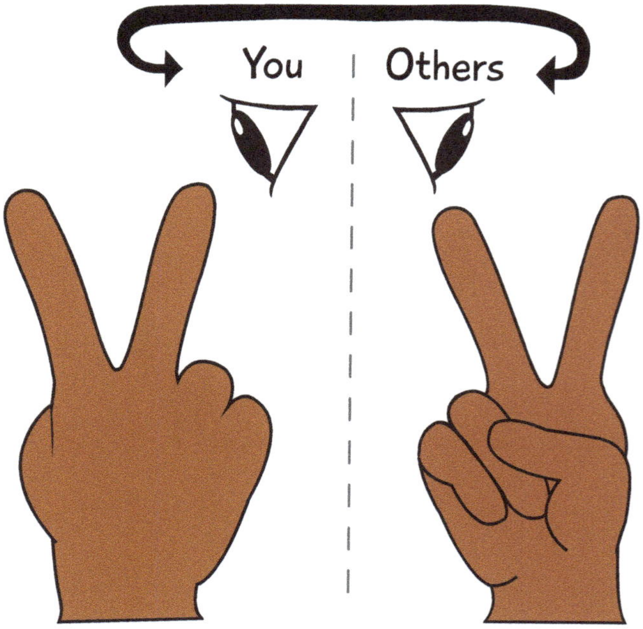

You   Others

1

V = V

= v

Violin   Vampire   Vegetables

Volcano   Vivid

Trace the dotted lines with a pencil or pen to finish the picture!

Let's practice the letter "V" now!

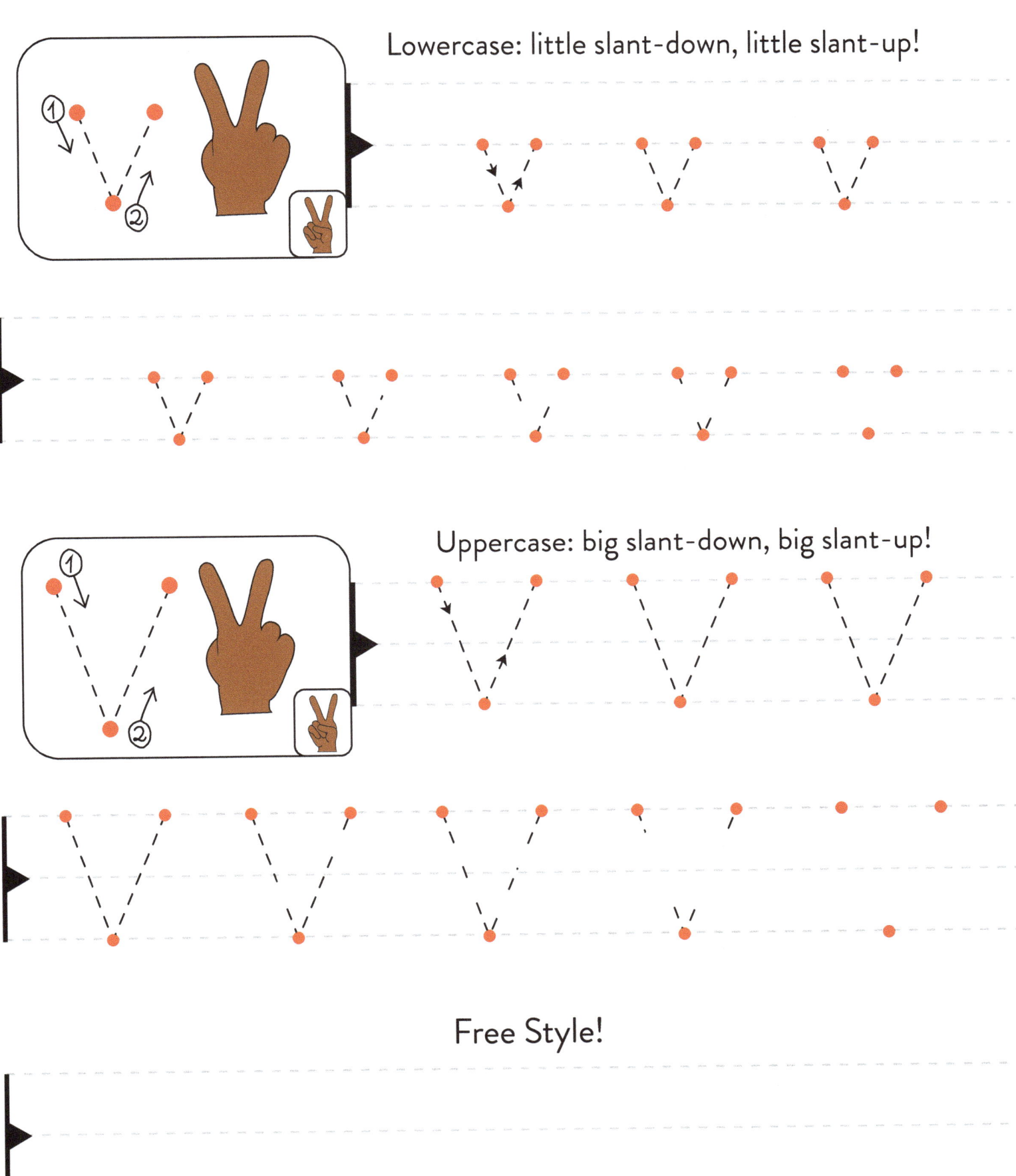

Lowercase: little slant-down, little slant-up!

Uppercase: big slant-down, big slant-up!

Free Style!

THIS IS THE LETTER "W": TRACE IT WITH YOUR FINGER

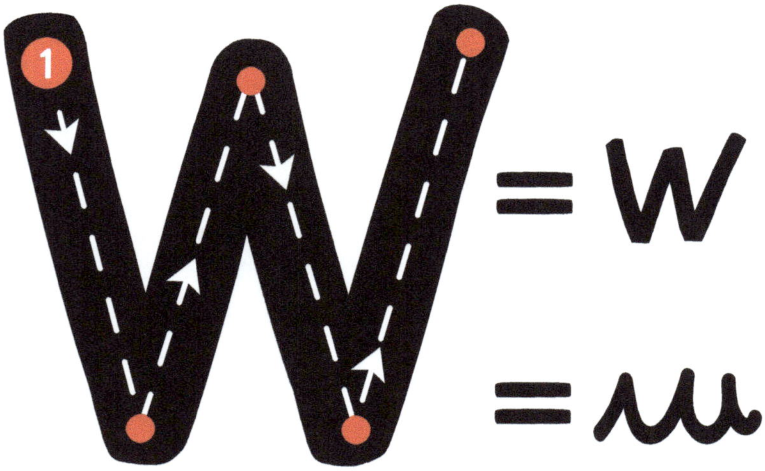

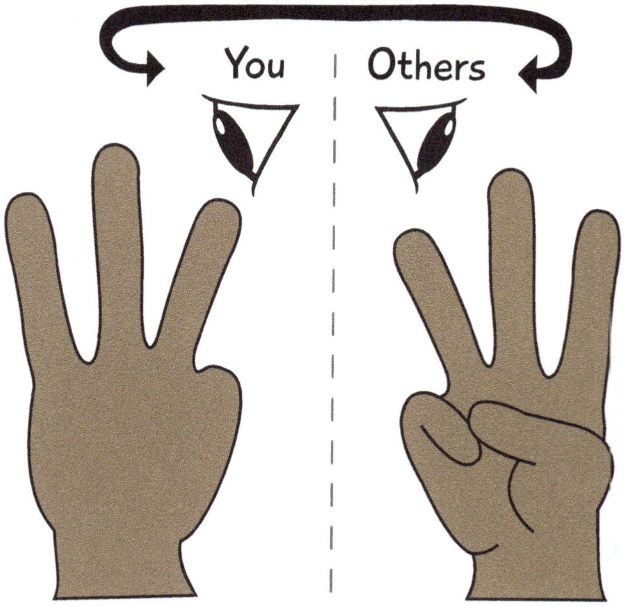

W = w

W = ᴍᴜ

You | Others

Whale   Window   Wallet

Wizard   Worm

Trace the dotted lines with a pencil or pen to finish the picture!

Let's practice the letter "W" now!

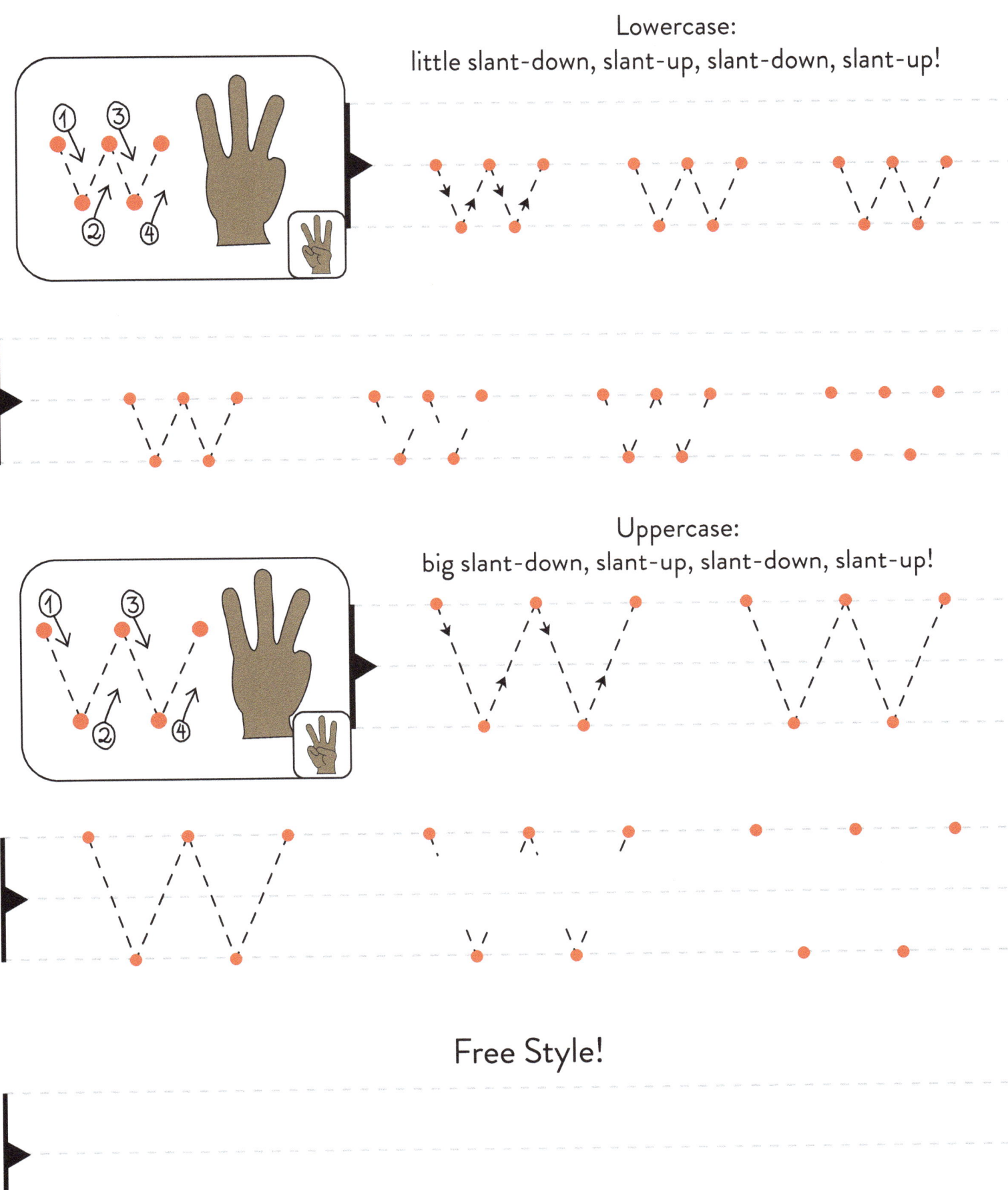

Lowercase:
little slant-down, slant-up, slant-down, slant-up!

Uppercase:
big slant-down, slant-up, slant-down, slant-up!

Free Style!

THIS IS THE LETTER "K": TRACE IT WITH YOUR FINGER

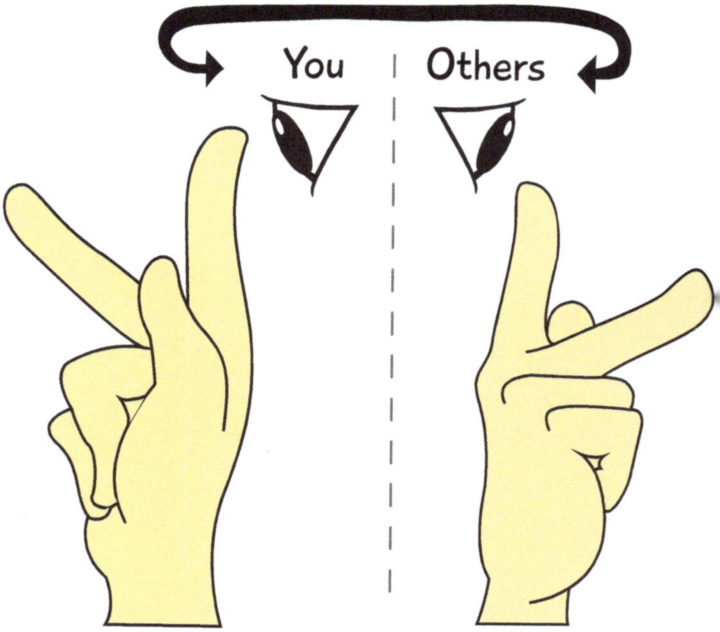

K = k

K = k

You | Others

Knife   Kick   Koala

Kitchen   Kite

Trace the dotted lines with a pencil or pen to finish the picture!

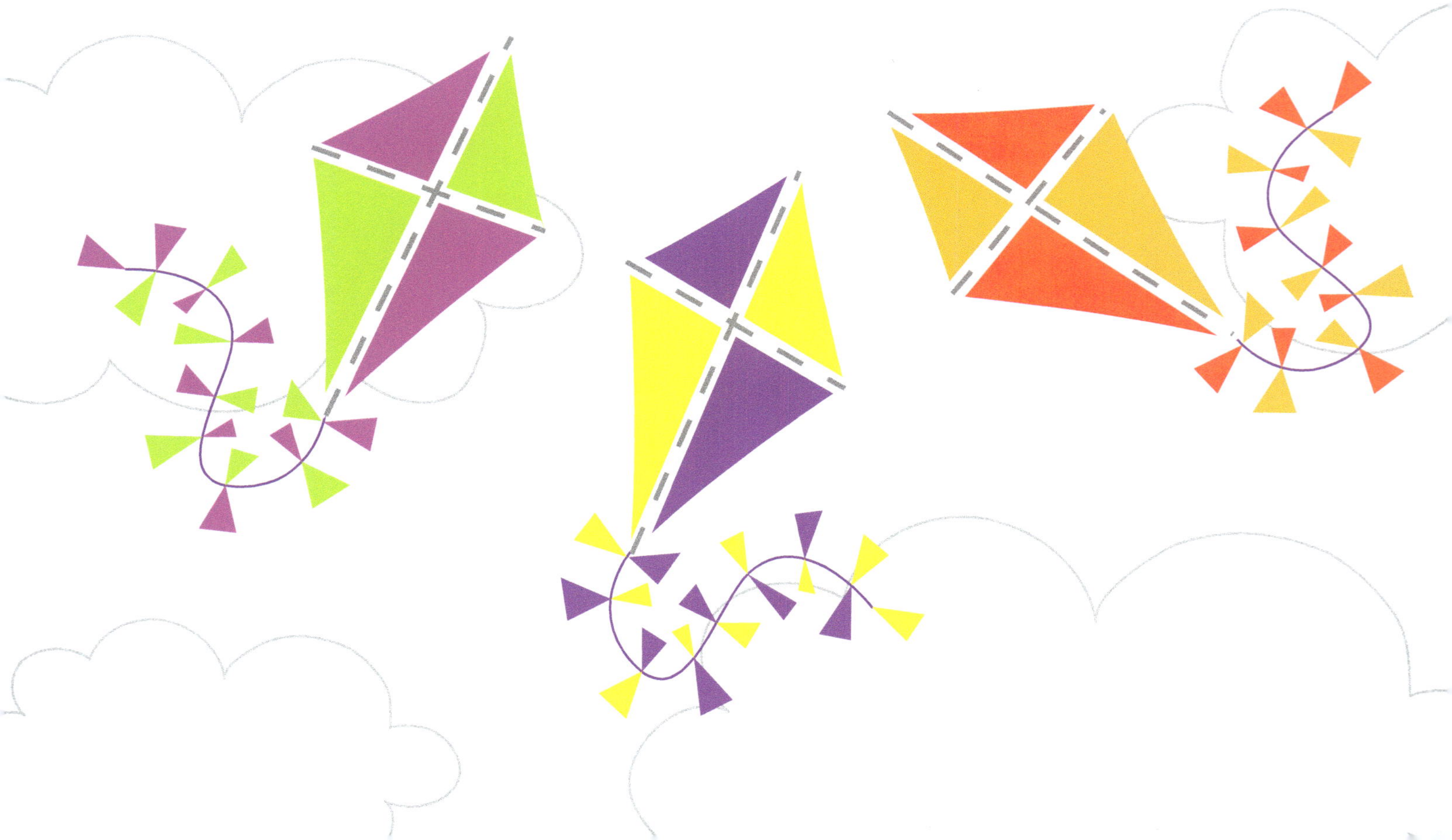

Let's practice the letter "K" now!

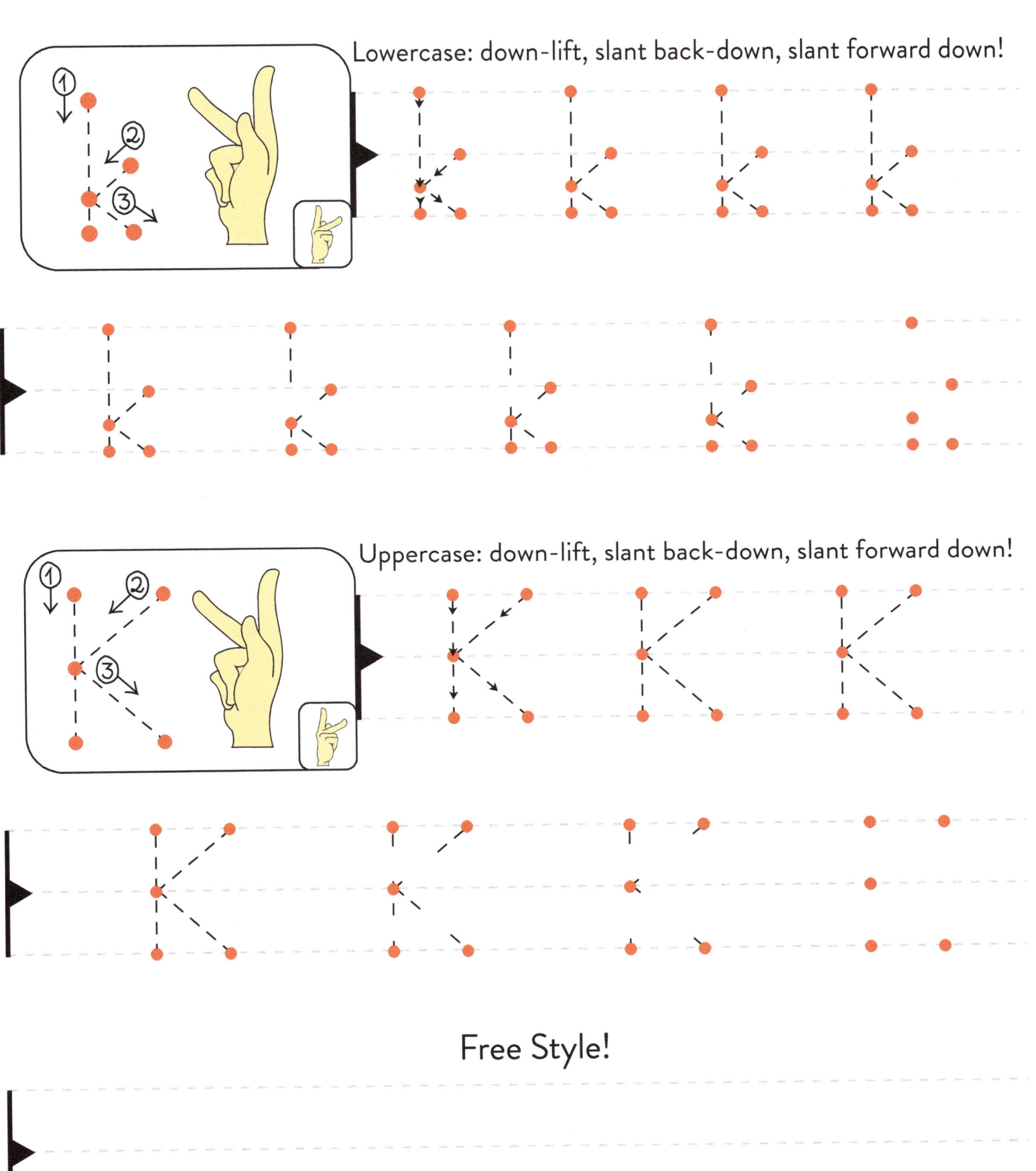

Lowercase: down-lift, slant back-down, slant forward down!

Uppercase: down-lift, slant back-down, slant forward down!

Free Style!

THIS IS THE LETTER "X": TRACE IT WITH YOUR FINGER

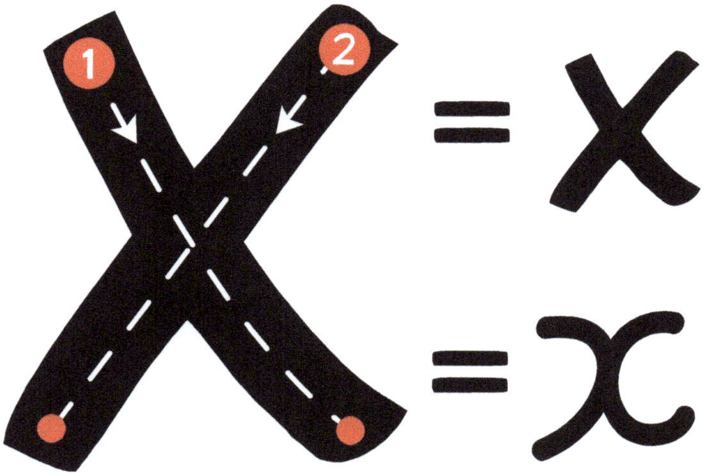

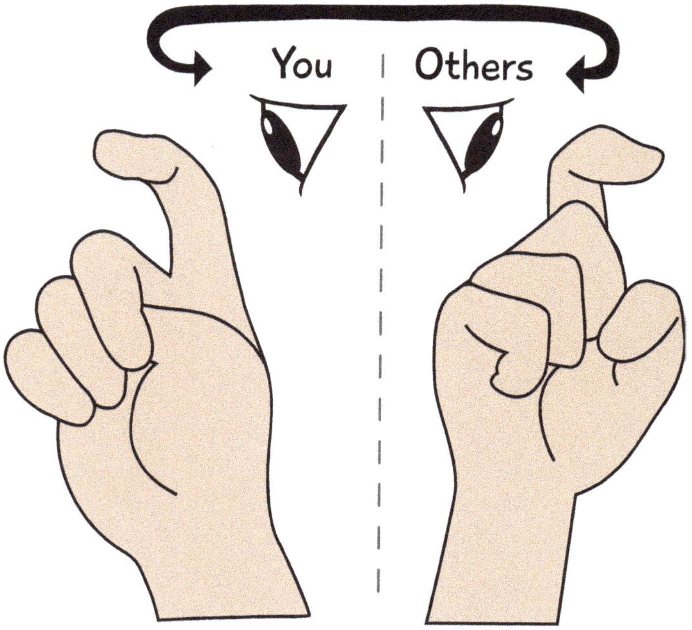

X = X
X = x

You | Others

Box
X-ray
Xylophone
Wax
Fix

Trace the dotted lines with a pencil or pen to finish the picture!

Let's practice the letter "X" now!

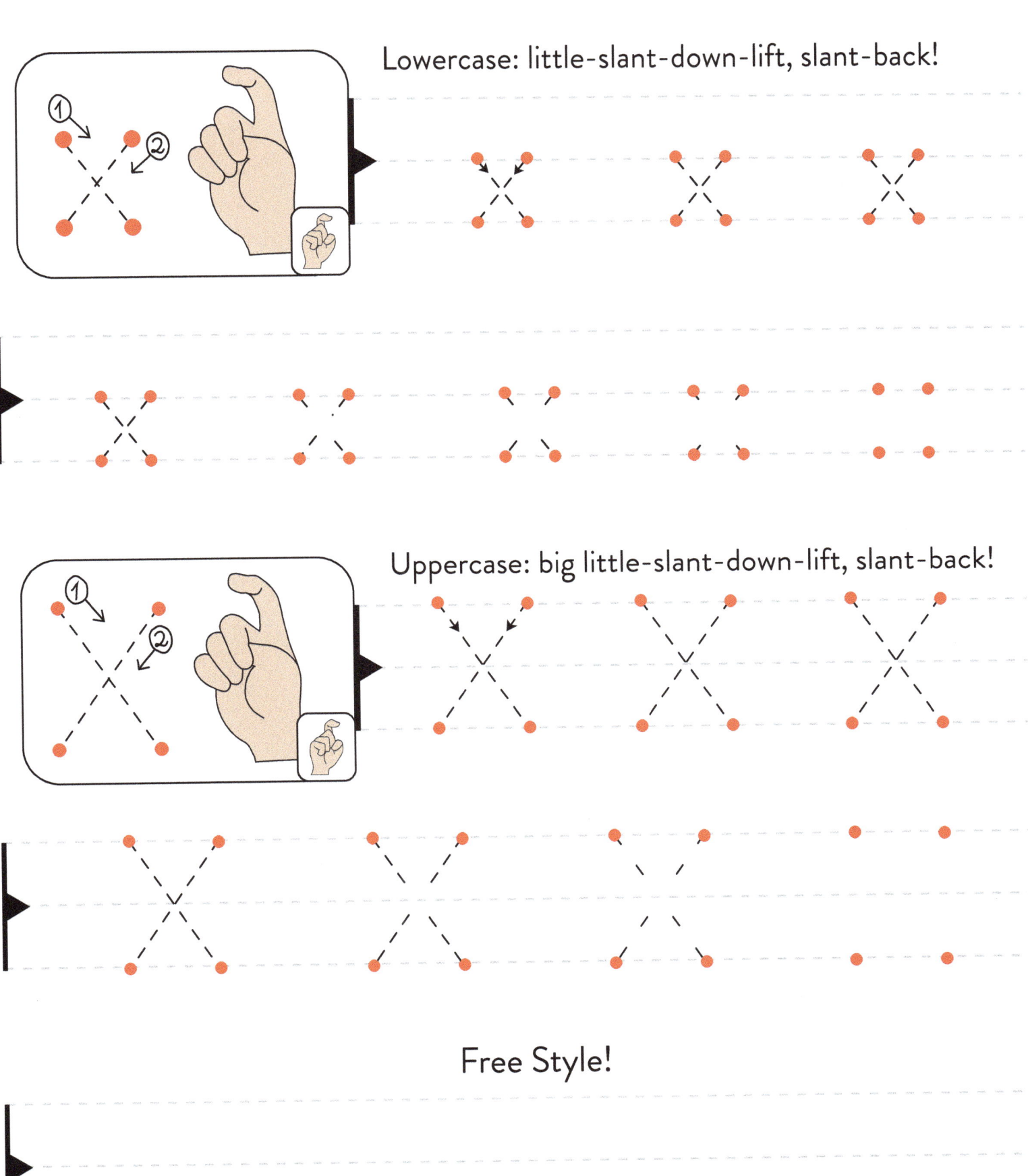

Lowercase: little-slant-down-lift, slant-back!

Uppercase: big little-slant-down-lift, slant-back!

Free Style!

THIS IS THE LETTER "Y": TRACE IT WITH YOUR FINGER

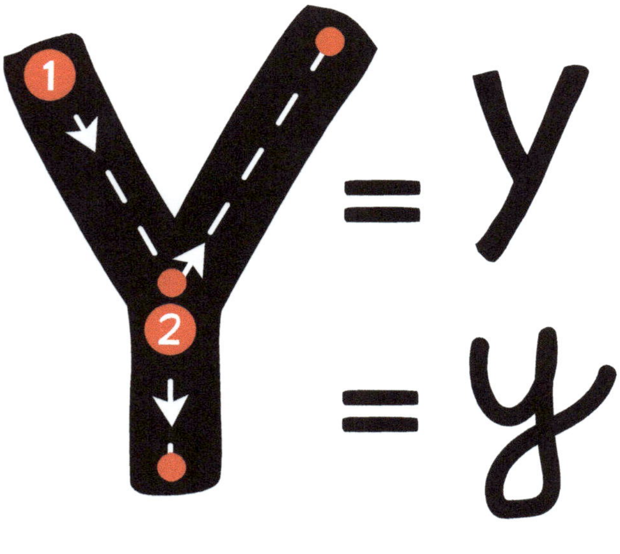

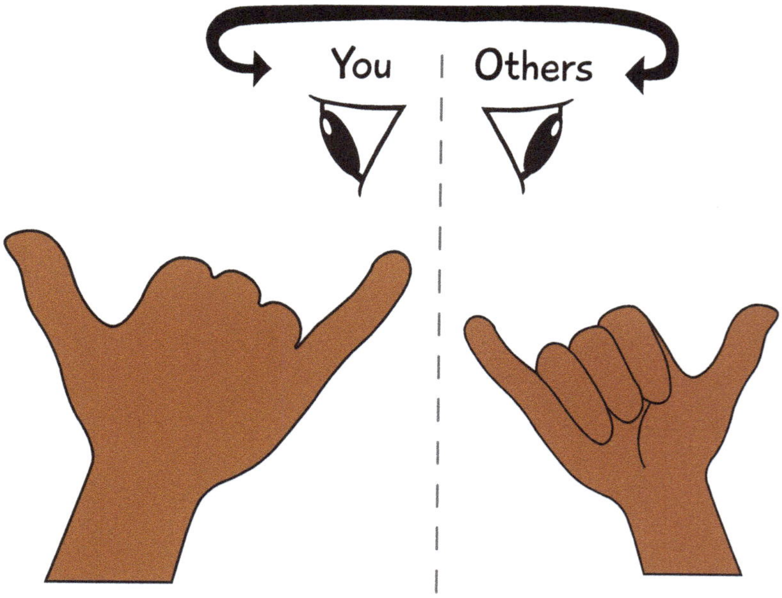

Y = y

Y = y

You | Others

Yacht

Yesterday

Yummy

Yellow

Yolk

Trace the dotted lines with a pencil or pen to finish the picture!

Let's practice the letter "Y" now!

Lowercase: slant down-lift, slant back!

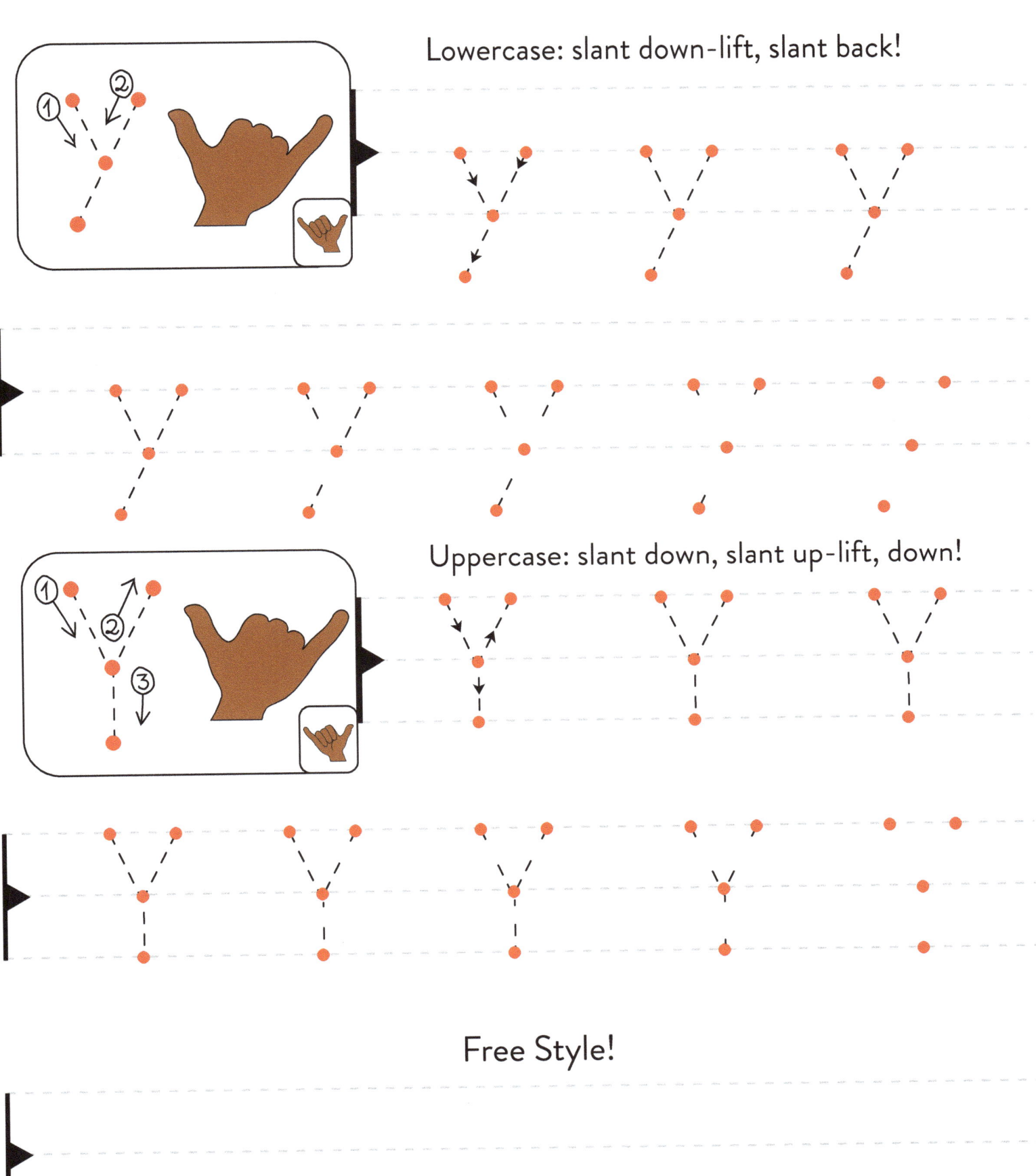

Uppercase: slant down, slant up-lift, down!

Free Style!

THIS IS THE LETTER "Z": TRACE IT WITH YOUR FINGER

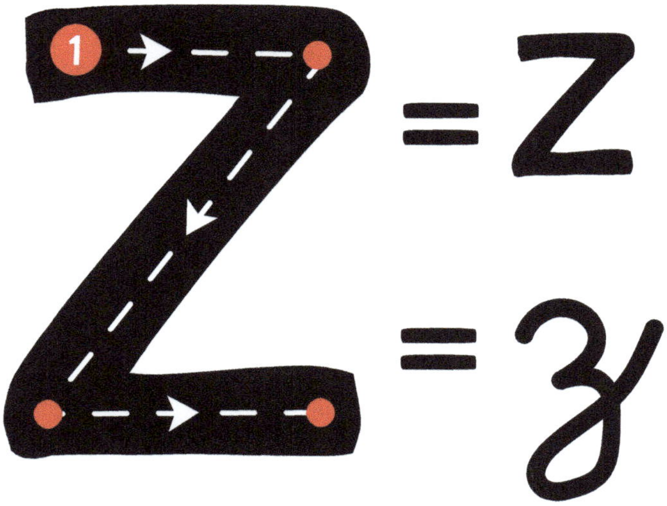

Z = Z

Z = ʒ

You | Others

Zombie   Zucchini   Zebra

Zig zag   Zero

Trace the dotted lines with a pencil or pen to finish the picture!

Let's practice the letter "Z" now!

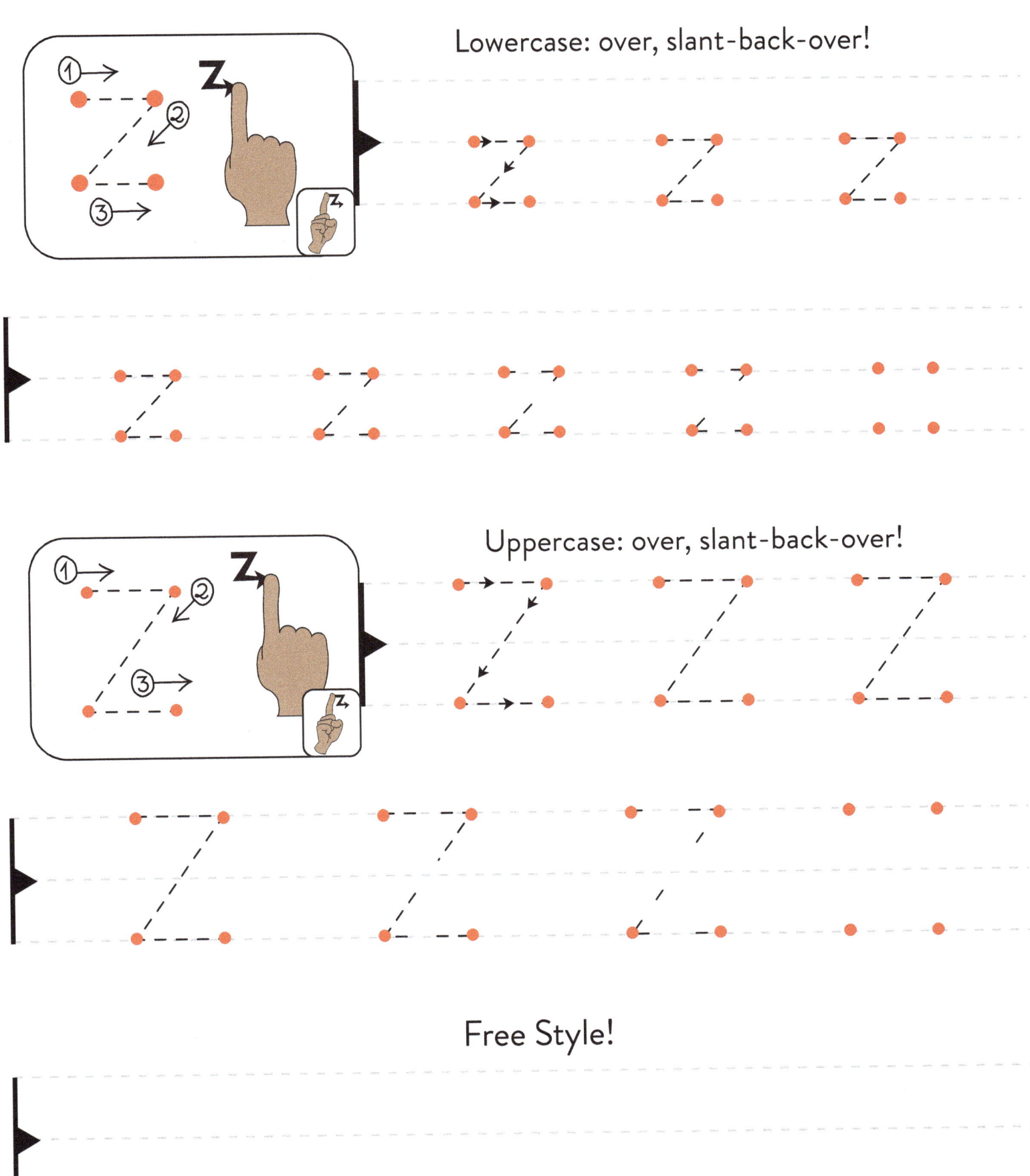

Lowercase: over, slant-back-over!

Uppercase: over, slant-back-over!

Free Style!

My Alphabet

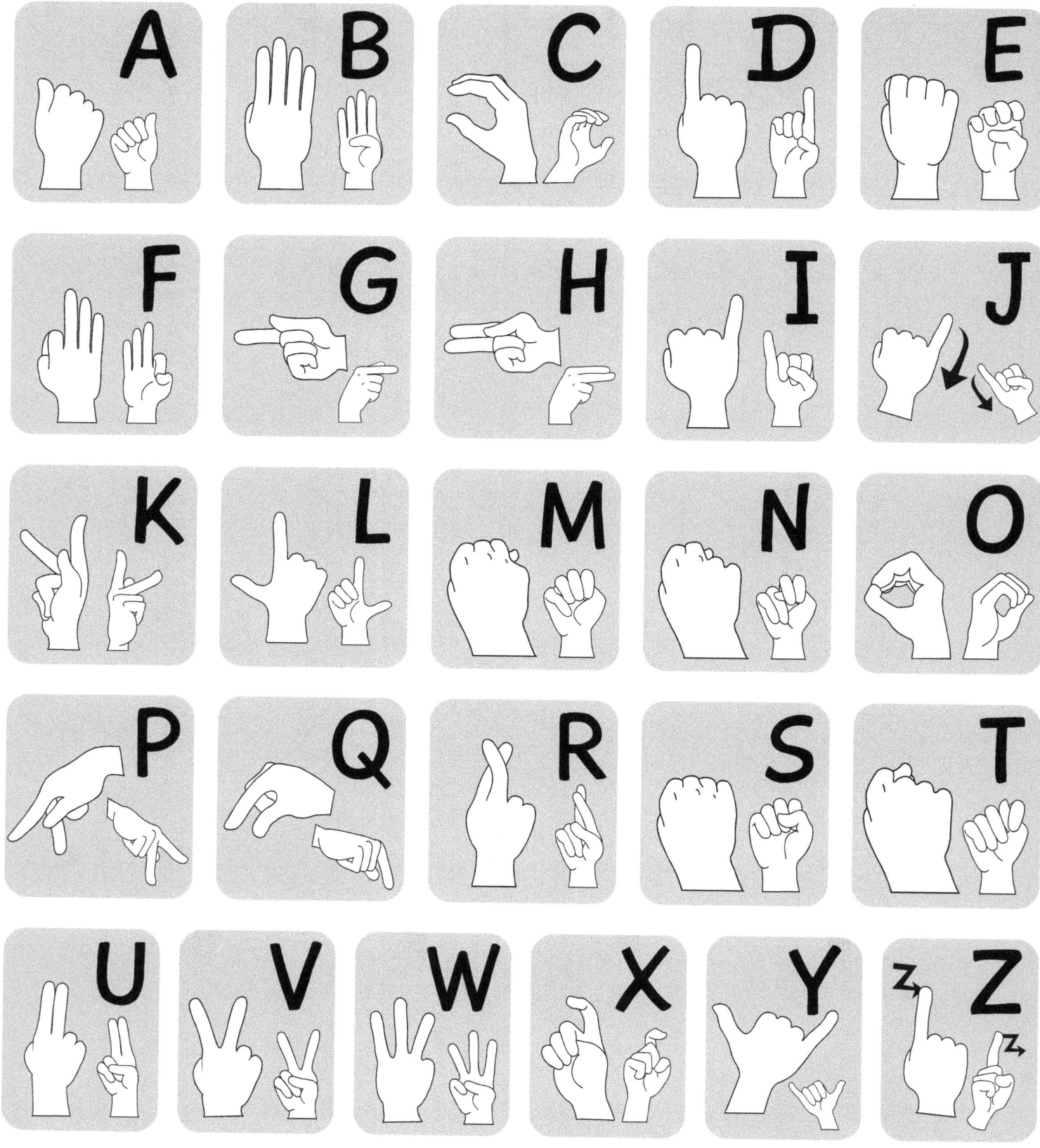

My Alphabet

Check some of my other books at:
www.amazon.com/author/kellelima

Scan this code with your phone!

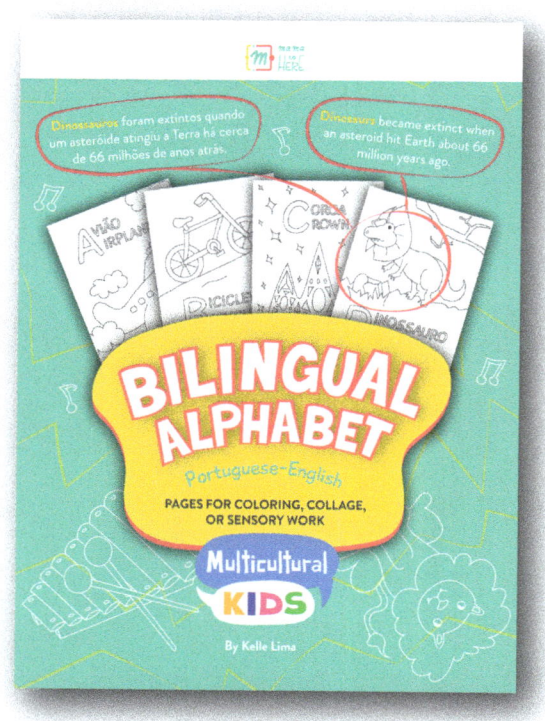

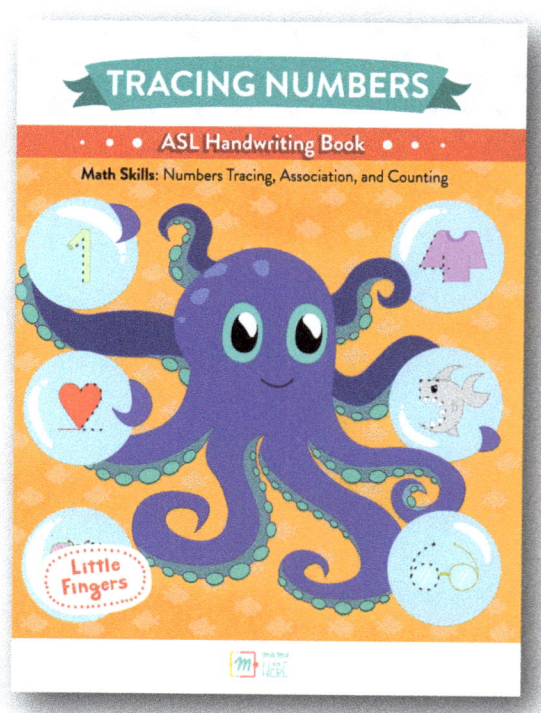

Hi there, I hope your learning journey has been great!
Did you enjoy this book?
Please consider leaving a positive review!

I would love to connect with you:

  @mamaishere2021

For FREE learning video resources, subscribe to my channel:

 bit.ly/Mamaishere